APPLYING PSYCHOLOGY to organisations

SHEILA HAYWARD

Series Editor: ROB McILVEEN

Hodder & Stoughton

A MEMBER OF THE HODDER HEADLINE GROUP

DEDICATION

This book is dedicated to Sharon, Phil, Claude, Jan and Peter – change agents who changed my life!

British Library Cataloguing in Publication Data

Hayward, Sheila
Applying Psychology to Organisations
1.Psychology, Industrial 2.Business enterprises -
Psychological aspects
I.Title II.Organisations
158.7

ISBN 0340 64758 2

First published 1996

Impression number	10	9	8	7	6	5	4	3	2	1
Year	1999	1998	1997	1996						

Typeset by Transet Ltd, Coventry, England.
Printed in Great Britain for Hodder & Stoughton Educational, a division of Hodder Headline Plc, 338 Euston Road, London NW1 3BH by Redwood Books, Trowbridge, Wilts

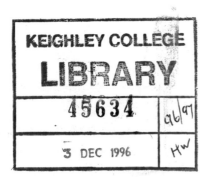

CONTENTS

PREFACE

This book aims to provide an introduction to key areas, research studies and applications of psychology in organisations. As such, it will be invaluable as a text for A-level Psychology students, and undergraduates who are commencing a module of Organisational Psychology. This, of course, is such a vast field that it would be impossible to cover all topics thoroughly in a volume of this size. An introductory level of knowledge of psychological theory is assumed, as this is an applied field; it takes up where theory leaves off and shows how psychology can be applied in organisations.

chapter one

WHAT IS ORGANISATIONAL PSYCHOLOGY?

CHAPTER OVERVIEW

This chapter aims to explain what is meant by the term 'organisational psychology' and to outline some structures and ways of functioning within organisations. Research methods applicable to organisational psychology are outlined; these are similar to core psychological methods, as organisational psychology is based on core psychological theories and concepts. Some early and current studies demonstrate ways in which psychology can be applied in organisations.

INTRODUCTION

The area of organisational psychology looks at the development and application of psychological theories in the workplace. In the past, the term 'occupational psychology' was used, but as the area has broadened, the title has changed. Occupational psychology focused on occupations or jobs, whereas organisational psychology examines the whole organisation where these jobs take place. A 'fitter' is an occupation; British Aerospace (organisation) employs fitters, but the work practices for the same occupation may differ from Ford Cars in terms of actions, responsibilities and work organisation.

Theories from many areas of psychology form the basis for work in organisational psychology. Attention, perception and cognition theories are important in designing job tasks within the human capacity and for drawing maximum attention to signals when things go wrong. Learning and memory theories can indicate the best training methods for jobs and work practices. Social psychology theories are applicable in the workplace: areas such as group cohesion, leadership, motivation, attitudes and attributions are all highly relevant to the workplace. Psychometrics, the measurement of human personality and cognitive functioning, is a growing field in organisational psychology, in the selection, training and team-building of personnel. Physiological psychology gives insight into the relationships between human physical and mental functioning at work, and is especially important in the identification of problem areas, such as stress. Organisational psychology is about turning theory into practice. At last, there is a way to 'sell' psychology – the old complaint used to be that we could not even give psychology away! As psychologists, we should have known that people do not appreciate what is given to them, they prefer to pay for it.

WHAT DOES AN ORGANISATIONAL PSYCHOLOGIST DO?

An organisational psychologist may work for either a large organisation or for a consultancy who will be called in to advise on specific problem areas. Psychologists are uniquely qualified to see the human factors involved in organisational problems. They may address questions such as 'How do I make the workers more productive?', and can say at the outset that bigger whips are not the answer, whereas providing more humane working conditions and improving work practices would optimise productivity. It may be necessary to redesign a work environment, re-structure job tasks or suggest better selection procedures for employees in the first place. This should be done with consideration for the psychology of the individual and the behaviour of the organisation as a whole – organisations differ as greatly as individuals.

THE NATURE AND STRUCTURE OF ORGANISATIONS

An organisation may be defined as a group with more or less constant membership, a purpose and a set of operating procedures. The 'membership' would be the people who work in the organisation, the 'structure' of the organisation would define their relationship to each other. The 'purpose' would be the goals of that particular organisation. These may be 'output goals', for example, producing cars. Linked with these may be 'societal goals' – ways in which the organisation plans to contribute to the wider community, for example by using materials which can be or have been recycled. These goals may well be contained in the organisation's mission statement, an explicit description of what the organisation aims to achieve. Other goals may be unstated, but exist nonetheless, in order to promote survival of the organisation. These goals underpin the organisation's 'personality' or 'culture'. (Organisational culture is discussed in Chapter 7.)

The structure of an organisation is related to the nature of that organisation; the structure necessary for a school is different from the structure necessary for running a manufacturing industry. Jobs are separated into groups of related activities, and these are frequently grouped within departments, with a departmental manager or head. Organisational strategic planning is usually the job of top management. Implementation of the plans is carried out by middle managers, and the planned tasks by the 'operating core' (see Figure 1.1).

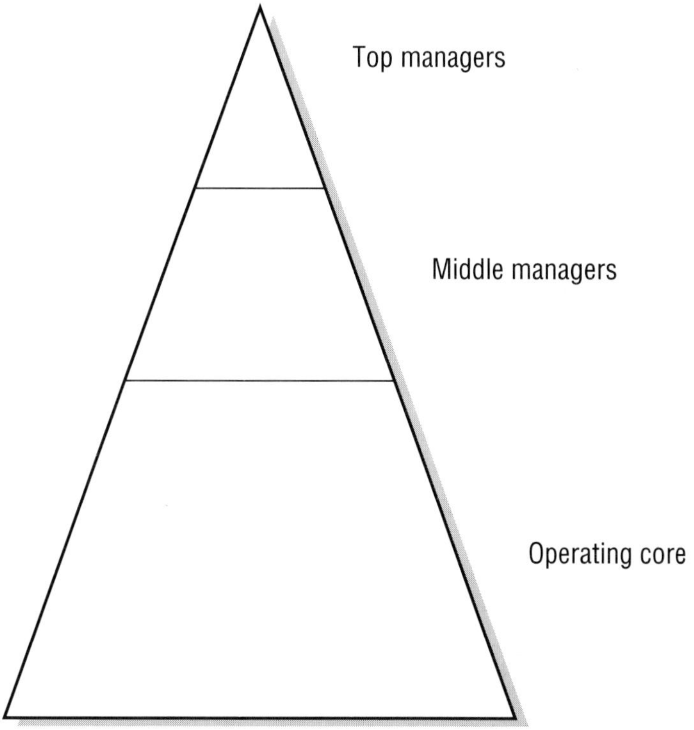

FIGURE 1.1 *Organisational structure: the structure of an organisation by divisions of labour*

Depending on the complexity of the organisation and the amount of differentiation in the jobs within it, there may be a number of 'layers' in the organisation's structure. A manufacturing company may have a 'tall structure', in other words a number of levels through which the chain of command passes (see Figure 1.2 overleaf).

An organisation where members of the workforce are all relatively autonomous (self-organising), each being 'expert' in his or her own field, may have a flat structure (see Figure 1.3 overleaf), where there may be only one or two levels.

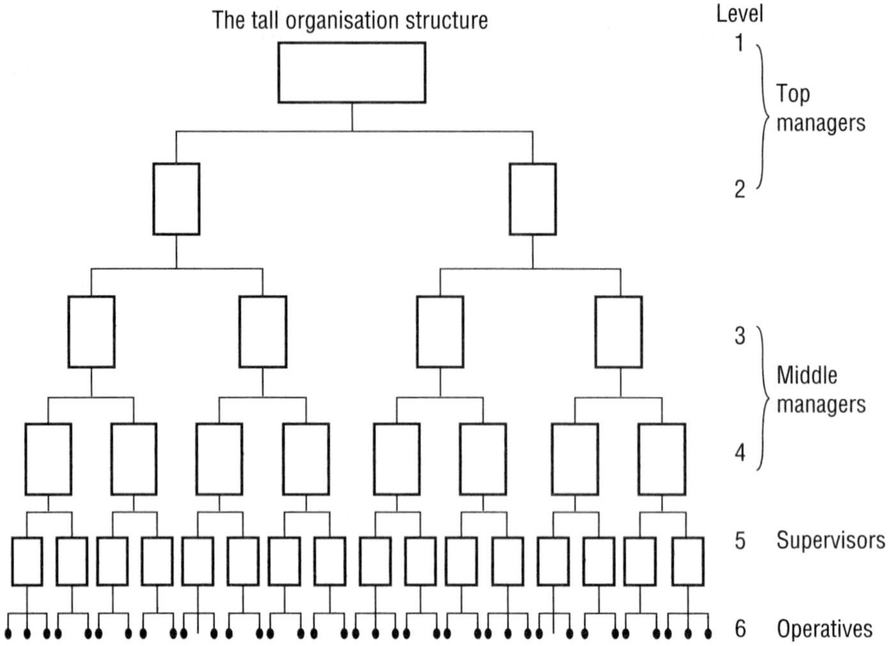

FIGURE 1.2 *Tall organisational structure. This type of structure is typical of traditional manufacturing industries*

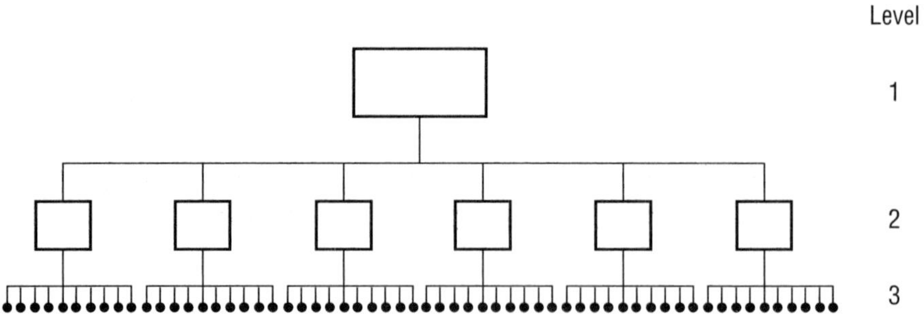

FIGURE 1.3 *Flat organisational structure: a school or college usually has a flat structure, with the headmaster or principal at Level 1, departmental heads at Level 2 and teaching staff at Level 3*

Power and decision-making

Everyone within an organisation has a degree of power, at least over the job they do. In most organisations, procedures are formalised and usually written down, hence the expression 'doing things by the book'. In **centralised**

organisations, decisions are made by top management, whereas in **decentralised organisations**, decisions may be made by group managers or supervisors, although top management still make the important policy decisions. The power relationship in an organisation is usually the inverse of its structure (see Figure 1.4).

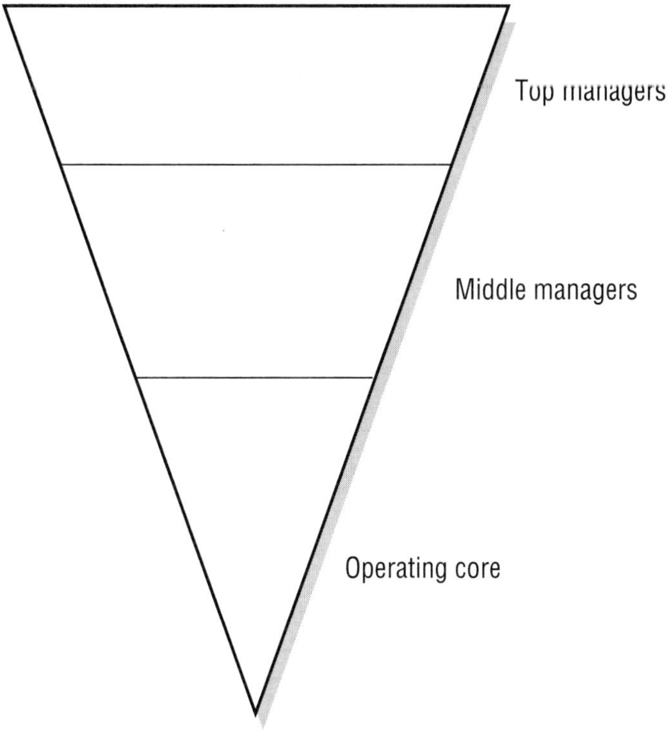

FIGURE 1.4 *The investiture of power in an organisation. Although there are fewer top managers in the organisation, the bulk of the power rests with them. Core operatives are numerically the greatest, but possess the least power*

Bureaucracies

Bureaucracies contain many levels of highly differentiated activities, with highly specialised jobs and often little or no communication upwards between the levels; communication is usually top-down. Decision-making is centralised and formal, with little or no delegation to middle or lower levels.

Bureaucracies have the advantage of being rational and orderly; everyone is treated equally. They are very effective in stable environments, but inflexible and unwieldy when circumstances change rapidly, as can happen nowadays with frequent technological advances. Working in a bureaucracy is often seen to be demotivating by employees, as the rigidity of the organisation presents little or no chance of innovation or promotion.

AREAS INVOLVING ORGANISATIONAL PSYCHOLOGISTS

Organisational psychologists may be asked to advise on any of the following areas, many of which are discussed at greater length in this book.

1 **Job analysis**
Deciding what a job actually consists of, in order to evaluate it or select the most appropriate personnel (more of this in Chapter 2). Even established jobs change over time, for example with the introduction of new technology. In Charles Dickens' time, in order to be a clerk, you had to have beautiful copperplate handwriting; that no longer appears in current job descriptions!
2 **Personnel selection**
Once the job is defined, it is necessary to find the right person, in order to maximise efficiency and to give that person job satisfaction. People will not stay in jobs where they do not 'fit', and constant changes of personnel are not cost-effective.
3 **Training**
Designing a training scheme for the skills identified as necessary for a specific job.
4 **Job satisfaction and the quality of work life**
This is important from the point of view of the employee; people do not go to work solely to earn money – they want to enjoy their jobs, too. An employer would want employees to enjoy work, as well as being productive.
5 **Motivation**
If people do not simply go to work for money, what is their motivation? What factors can improve work motivation?
6 **Improving organisational structure**
The structure of an organisation defines how work is organised, and how relationships function within it. From time to time, whole organisations need restructuring.
7 **Human factors and working conditions**
Designing optimum conditions for the person/machine interface can benefit both the worker and the organisation, in terms of health, satisfaction and productivity.

8 Performance appraisal
The work performance of employees is often given formal appraisal. These systems need to be carefully designed in order to be fair and effective.

9 Leadership
Effective leadership is necessary in industry and commerce, in order to compete in a global environment. Potential leaders need to be identified and may need specialist training.

10 Workgroups
Not many people work in isolation. Work practices may be formally organised into productivity groups. Other work groups may be less formal, with changing membership.

11 Facilitating organisational change
Changes in organisations may mean upheaval for employees; sometimes the fear of upheaval is greater than the actual event. Organisational psychologists can advise on change and smooth the pathway.

12 Counselling
Many companies employ counsellors in the workplace who are trained to deal with work-related as well as other problems. Counsellors may also be brought in to facilitate organisational change.

13 Stress and stress management
The recognition of work-related stress and its alleviation is the job of a specially trained organisational psychologist.

14 Evaluating work practices
Usually the job of an external consultant, bringing a fresh point of view into the organisation, work practices can be evaluated and, if necessary, updated. An organisational psychologist can also advise on consumer behaviour patterns, which are likely to change over time, without organisations realising how detrimental this can be to their business.

PROBLEMS OF STUDYING PEOPLE AT WORK

People are sometimes uncomfortable about being watched while at work. They may equate psychologists with the 'time-and-motion' man of previous years, who watched for a while and then told you that it was possible to work faster. People are naturally wary, especially during an era of 'downsizing', or reducing employee numbers by reallocating jobs between fewer people. There may be questions from employees, such as,

'Are you the time-and-motion study expert?', 'Are you going to take my job away? or 'What's in it for me?'

One of the major problems which occurs (as with all observation studies) is that, by observing behaviour, you may well be changing it. Evidence that this happened was provided by the Hawthorne (1939) studies (see Box 1.1), one of the first systematic work studies to be documented.

Box 1.1 The Hawthorne Effect

A series of experimental studies was carried out at the Hawthorne plant of the Western Electric Company, in Illinois, USA, over a period of two and a half years.

A group of five employees in the relay assembly section had their working conditions systematically changed, in order to try and identify optimal conditions. Factors changed included: level of lighting, heating, humidity, food consumed, work/sleep hours. With each change, productivity output increased and remained at that level, even when conditions reverted to normal! This was not what the investigators were expecting, and reasons were sought.

One reason suggested was the change in social environment; they were suddenly important as a group of employees, and their opinion was asked on work matters. Absenteeism had also declined, and this was attributed to increased feelings of group cohesiveness.

The outcome of this study became known as 'The Hawthorne Effect'. The mere fact that you are studying something changes it. These studies have been reanalysed many times, and different reasons for the outcome suggested. However, whatever the reasons, the 'effect' still occured and was documented.

RESEARCH METHODS AND ANALYSIS IN ORGANISATIONAL PSYCHOLOGY

In order to improve work practices, productivity, work conditions and all the other factors involved in organisational life, it is necessary to make a systematic, empirical study. Findings can then be presented to the parties interested in the most effective functioning of that organisation, who are generally not psychologists. As a rule, it is difficult to generalise findings from one organisation to another, because of their individual differences (just as with people).

Research methods employed are similar to other areas of psychology with experimental methods, surveys and observational methods being used most often, sometimes in combination with each other, to give a comprehensive picture.

1 Experimental methods

This term implies that the researcher is deliberately isolating one factor (known as the **independent variable**), in order to measure its effect on a specific outcome (the **dependent variable**). The researcher produces operational definitions for each of these, which are working definitions specific to the study in hand. To give a simple example, a company may wish to investigate whether employees' attitudes to work influence their productivity. The operational definition of the independent variable may be 'total score on the Work Attitudes scale', while a productivity measure would be determined for the dependent variable.

Experimental methods are often used for pinpointing specific cause-and-effect behaviours, either as a **field experiment**, in the workplace itself, or as a **laboratory experiment**, in conditions set up by the experimenter. The purpose may be to identify which are essential job behaviours, and must therefore be included in any training programme, or to identify under which (simulated) work conditions the job can best be carried out. In addition, a method often utilised in the workplace is the **quasi-experimental design**. This is where differences occur naturally between two groups of workers, and comparisons can be made between them. For example, a manufacturing company may have two units, both producing exactly the same components, but using different work practices. Investigation into such variables as work practices, employee selection procedures and management style would yield useful information as to reasons for outcome measures such as productivity and quality. Changes could be recommended if one manufacturing unit was found to be significantly more effective, due to differences in one or more variables.

Experimental methods may be used for the evaluation of new procedures, to demonstrate that they are more effective than previous procedures. This is often the case with training programmes, where cost-effectiveness is of great importance. It is essential to know whether six weeks' training is more effective than three weeks' training, or whether no training at all provides equivalent on-the-job performance.

Groups which are designate as **control groups** (for comparison purposes) should only differ from experimental groups in respect of the independent variable; all other conditions should be held constant.

The usual criticisms applied to experimental research apply in organisations. People behave differently under experimental conditions, and the experimenter may not have allowed for all extraneous variables. The strengths of experiments include the isolation of cause and effect, and the control and objectivity of the study. Replicability would, of course, be limited to similar organisations.

2 Observational studies

Observational methods are often used where it is impracticable to use an experimental study. Observation is also used as a preliminary to experiments, in order to identify variables and suggest hypotheses which may be investigated by experiments at a later date.

Direct observation may be carried out by researchers in order to study work behaviours, either of individuals or of group processes, if these are important to the area of study. As with most observational studies, checklists of potentially observable behaviours are prepared in advance (perhaps after preliminary observation and discussion), so that a written record of total observations can be kept. As mentioned earlier, the observer effect is liable to occur: behaviour is changed simply because it is being observed. This effect can be minimised by not commencing the statistical observations until employees are used to the observer's presence.

Covert observation is not encouraged in the workplace; it is considered unethical to carry out systematic observations at work on people who are unaware that this is happening. For similar reasons, participant observation (i.e. where the observer performs similar tasks to those being observed) is not carried out nowadays in the workplace; in addition, jobs are now often so complex, it would be an expensive process to train a participant observer.

3 Surveys

Sometimes the required information can be elicited in the workplace by means of questionnaires or interviews. This is particularly appropriate if the information required is factual, rather than behavioural, or if it relates to feelings or attitudes of employees.

Questionnaires have to be constructed carefully, using appropriate terminology, and avoiding ambiguous questions. The advantage of using questionnaire surveys is that a large number of participants can be involved, eliciting a great deal of information without high costs. The disadvantages are that people do not always do what they say they do, so the information may contain a degree of inaccuracy. Sometimes it is an advantage to allow questionnaires to be returned anonymously, especially if individuals feel that their replies might prejudice their work positions.

4 Action research

Frequently, in organisational psychology, a research project undertaken for an organisation involves the use of more than one method of research, in order to answer all the questions posed by a real-world situation. This is done in order to take action on the findings or, if the complete answer is not found, to investigate still further. Action research is a process of investigation, rather than a method. This process may involve any number of investigations, using the same or different methods of investigation (see Figure 1.5).

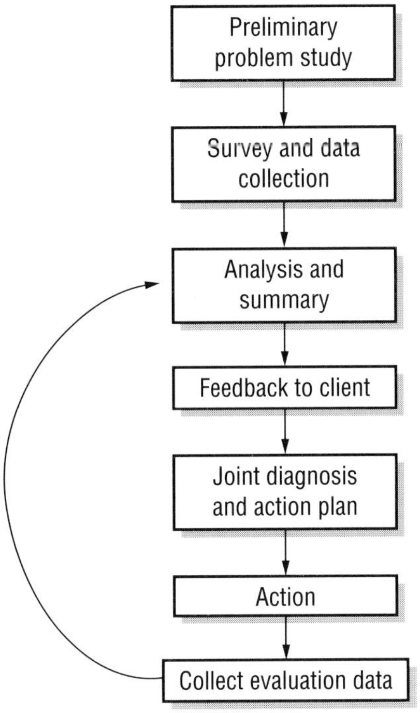

FIGURE 1.5 *The action research process*

The first step is problem diagnosis, which is different for each organisation, so the psychologist must take some time understanding the real problems. Preliminary investigations are discussed with representatives of the organisation, who join in the diagnosis and plan the next action. Outcomes are evaluated, and if the problems are not entirely solved, or new problems emerge, the cycle is repeated.

The methodology for one such research project is described in Box 1.2 below.

Box 1.2 Research methods to determine the design of flight-deck systems in aircraft

As aircraft technology becomes more complex, so do the flight-deck systems controlling those aircraft. It is essential that the design of these systems is as user-friendly as possible. With this aim in view, a joint study was undertaken by British Airways, the University of Bristol Psychology and Aerospace Engineering Departments and Smiths Aerospace Industries of Cheltenham, who engineer the instrumentation for avionics flight decks.

Research proceeded as follows:

1 **Familiarisation activities.** These fell into two categories:
   (i) literature searches in appropriate areas, to find out what had already been discovered about flight decks, and making contact with people who had performed similar investigations
   (ii) physical involvement, which consisted mainly of observational studies: spending time on the flight decks, observing, both during flight and in stationary aircraft; finding out about flight system components and how the system works.
2 **Structured interviews.** These elicited expert knowledge from flight-deck personnel as to what was important on the flight deck, for example what would happen in certain situations, whether any problems had been encountered with any system or components. As interviews are resource-hungry and time-consuming, both for interviewer and interviewee, only a percentage of staff were interviewed (one might call this a 'pilot study'!) Good interpersonal skills are necessary here.
3 **Design a questionnaire.** This was sent to all flight-deck personnel employed by the company to elicit a wide body of information on the items found to be important during the structured interviews.
4 **Analysis of the resultant data.** Data consists of the answers to the questionnaires. A report can then be supplied to the organisation, and design recommendations made.
5 **Verification exercise.** A check on the accuracy of the findings was made by returning to the respondents of the survey and asking them to confirm the findings.

(Noyes, Starr and Rankin, 1996)

The above study is an ergonomics (or Human Factors) study; this area of work is described in Chapter 5.

LEGISLATION AND LITIGATION

A great deal of legislation (laws) relate to work and work practices. These are specific to each country; legislation in the United States, for example, is not the same as in the United Kingdom. Legislation defines work hours and practices, safety procedures, areas of fairness and discrimination. The UK is now in alignment with much of the European (EU) legislation, but has not adopted all recommendations as yet; for example, there is still no legal minimum wage in the UK. Areas which often concern organisational psychologists are Health and Safety (discussed in Chapter 5) and Equal Opportunities (in Chapters 2 and 4).

Litigation is the process of taking legal action against someone who has broken the law, resulting in harm to you (either physical, monetary or psychological). The law is being increasingly invoked against employers in matters of ill-health caused by bad work practices, unfair discrimination or unfair dismissal. Employers may take legal action against employees who steal goods or give away valuable industrial or commercial information gained whilst in their employment. Litigation has also been pursued against organisational psychologists (mainly in the USA so far) over matters such as giving an inappropriate test in job selection procedures, which resulted in that person not being selected for the job. Litigation in the field of employment is an advancing problem, and one of which organisational psychologists should be aware.

SUMMARY

This chapter has briefly outlined the role of organisational psychology today. The structure of organisations relates to the purpose of that organisation and also has bearing on the decision-making processes within it. Research methods used in organisational psychology are linked to real-world problems.

chapter two

PERSONNEL SELECTION

CHAPTER OVERVIEW

This chapter explores the necessity for careful selection of personnel, as a three-stage process: pre-recruitment, recruitment and selection. It looks at the methods used to analyse jobs in order to clarify what is expected of the job holder. With changing technology, jobs may change and old job descriptions become out of date. Methods of recruiting and subsequently selecting the right people for those jobs are discussed, together with the importance of work to the individual.

INTRODUCTION

Many organisations spend a great deal of time and money on personnel recruitment and selection. They must find this cost-effective, or they would not do it.

From the organisation's point of view, in order to fulfil the organisational goals, they need someone who will:

- get the job done efficiently
- maintain or increase production of that job area
- show potential for development towards promotion (many organisations prefer to promote from within, rather than recruit externally)
- 'fit' the job well – a good person/job fit is thought to lead to lower staff turnover and absenteeism, thereby reducing costs.

From the individual's point of view, he or she may like a job which:

- uses available skills or previous training
- provides an adequate income
- provides job satisfaction
- develops the individual's potential and abilities
- provides adequate challenge at the level desired.

These are generalisations; not all the points will apply to all individuals or all organisations.

Before recruitment

Job analysis and job design

Before recruitment, any vacancy which occurs may need to be re-analysed, in order to establish what the job actually constitutes. Jobs do not stay the same over time; as raw materials, tools and technology change, so jobs adapt. Job analysis is necessary before a job description can be drawn up, which would then be sent to applicants.

There are a number of job analysis methods which can be used. Frequently, a combination of information is taken from observations, interviews, surveys and previously existing data.

Observations

These can be made of the present job incumbents at work and job tasks can be observed. These are the actual actions and processes which the individual executes. This will yield information as to how that job is currently undertaken although this is not necessarily how the job could or should be done. The individual concerned may have adopted some work practices which are not as effective as they could be, perhaps not utilising new machinery to its fullest, or the individual may be 'cutting corners', which could result in loss of quality or lack of safety. If a number of employees are observed, all of whom perform the same jobs, then a range of measures can be taken, which would yield greater information. However, this still only tells you how the job is done at the moment, and gives no indication of the thought processes preceding the actions.

Interviews

These may be carried out, not only with job incumbents, but also with others who come into contact with that job. Interviewers may ask the reasons for actions taken while performing job tasks. Supervisors or subordinates may also be asked questions concerning what they think constitutes the job under analysis. These replies may be integrated into an overall analysis. Interviews may be unstructured, where the interviewer asks questions which are often derived from previous answers, or structured, when prepared questions are used. Careful use of interpersonal skills is needed to ensure that the interviewee does not feel threatened; this could result in inaccurate information being given.

Surveys

These may need to be taken if a large number of people need to give information. This may be necessary if a number of jobs are being analysed, due to expansion or reorganisation. Prepared questionnaires can be distributed and analysed without it being too costly a process.

Existing structured job analysis questionnaires are available. One of the most extensively researched is the Position Analysis Questionnaire (PAQ) developed by McCormick, Jeanneret and Meacham (1972). This has questions divided into six categories: job context, work output, mental processes, information output, relationships with other people and other job characteristics. The PAQ gives comprehensive information, which can be systematically analysed to give an accurate picture of the job.

Existing data

This sort of information on a number of jobs is available from various different sources. For example, secretarial agencies can give basic information about the number of words per minute which can be typed by different levels of secretarial staff. This may be a more objective method than collecting data from existing job incumbents.

Job evaluation

Once a job has been analysed, it can be evaluated in terms of what the job is worth, how much salary should be offered, whether a car is necessary and at what level in the organisation the job is seen to exist. The job will be weighed up in relation to other jobs deemed to be of comparable worth, that is to say, jobs which are similar in content or status. Job evaluation has to be decided before the job can be advertised.

Is job analysis effective?

Methods of carrying out job analysis were evaluated for effectiveness by experienced job analysts and reported by Levine et al. (1983). The study found that all job analysis tasks are seen as effective in different situations, but the use of multiple methods of job analysis has been found to be most effective in providing comprehensive analysis.

Job design and job specification

When job analysis has been carried out, a job specification can be drawn up. This specifies all the tasks to be carried out in the job. If the analysis has been made for a job not yet in existence (perhaps for a new company or one in the process of reorganisation), then job design will precede job specification.

Careful job design ensures that all the tasks can be carried out by the same person, in the work time allocated.

Job description

A job description can be drawn up following job analysis. This will include the job specification and probably a person specification as well. This indicates the personal attributes which are considered necessary for the job. These may be recognised qualifications, such as a specified degree, relevant certificates or a Heavy Goods Vehicle licence, plus personal qualities seen as important in that job, such as an ability to get on well with other people. Whatever is included in the person specification must be demonstrated to be relevant to the job; it is no longer permissible for employers to list their personal preferences.

RECRUITMENT

Once an organisation has a clear analysis of the job and the personnel required, recruitment can begin. The aim of recruitment is to find an individual who will work well in the job, be happy in the job and stay with the organisation, thereby reducing staff turnover and the costs involved in this. In addition, it is expensive for an organisation to be constantly training new staff.

The aim of recruitment is not simply to attract *as many* applicants as possible (which in these times of high unemployment may run into many hundreds, all of which would require screening), but to attract *appropriate* applicants. There are a number of methods of recruitment; the more usual ones are outlined below.

External advertisements

Advertisements may be placed in appropriate papers or journals. Specialised journals may be used for specialist jobs, local newspapers for non-specialist jobs. These are now bound by Equal Opportunities legislation, which means that they must not contain discriminating statements with regard to gender or race of applicants. In the USA, it is not permitted to discriminate on the grounds of age, but this is still legal in Britain. There is allowance for what is called 'positive discrimination' in companies where it is felt that people with disabilities and of certain ethnic groups or gender groups are under-represented. Applications from these groups may be encouraged, especially if the post seems to require this. You may see job advertisements which state 'Applications are invited from ethnic minorities, as these are under-represented in this organisation'. If an advertisement specifically asks for a male or a female applicant, the organisation must be able to demonstrate that this is necessary. Males as well as females are able to protest against unfair discrimination on the grounds of gender.

Advertisement contents will include: a brief description of the job requirements, benefits offered (wages, company car, etc.) and possibly a brief description of the organisation, together with the required procedure for applicants (they may have to write a letter of application or request an application form).

Current employee referrals

Another method of recruitment is by word of mouth, asking existing employees if they know of someone who would like the job. This is not as haphazard a method as it sounds, as it assumes that existing employees will know others who are like themselves, and if existing employees fit the organisation well, their friends will also fit. Gorlin (1982) surveyed a number of organisations, and they reported that most of their clerical and production employees were obtained in this way. The disadvantage of this method is that organisations eventually would consist of all the same 'type' of individuals, so this method of recruitment needs to be supplemented with other methods from time to time.

Internal recruitment

Advertising jobs within the organisation means that the employees' attributes and abilities are already known, to a certain extent. For the organisation, it removes some of the uncertainty of recruiting externally. For the employees, it is encouraging to think that promotion or access to other jobs is available within the organisation. If the job represents a promotion for the individual, there is still some risk that, although they were able to perform at one level, the next level may be just too difficult. Individuals who have been promoted beyond their capacity may well become subject to pressures, strain and possibly stress. The organisation may find that the individual's productivity is reduced as a result.

Box 2.1 Reliability and validity in selection procedures

In psychology, when we talk about validity, we are usually asking whether a test or questionnaire really tests what it says it is testing. Do intelligence tests, for example, really test intelligence? In personnel selection procedures, the question asked is, 'Is this procedure really selecting the right person for the job?'

Obviously the term 'right person' needs some qualification; what are the criteria for this? As all jobs may have a long list of different criteria, two are usually selected which will apply to most jobs: job tenure (the length of time a person stays in the job) and job performance (how well the person subsequently performs in the job). Therefore, if a study says that a particular selection procedure had high validity, it means the people selected by that method either stayed a long time in their jobs, or performed well, or both. What is actually being sought is a prediction that the person will be successful once in the job; this is predictive validity.

Reliability in psychology means that the test performs in the same way (reliably) each time you use it. In personnel selection, it has the same meaning: that a specific method of selection will produce the same results (equivalent standard of personnel) each time. Ideally, this would be coupled with high validity to produce a high standard of selection.

Selection procedures

A number of different selection procedures are available. Which ones are to be used will depend on (a) the job offered, (b) the method of recruitment used, (c) the number of applications received.

Standard application forms

An application form is usually a part of the selection procedure for any sizeable organisation, with standard questions on name, address, date of birth, education and previous work experience. Legislation does not allow for questions to be asked about the individual's religion, race and any disability, although these may be asked for, on a separate sheet for data purposes. They should not, however, be a basis for selection – answering these questions is optional.

Preliminary screening is often from the application forms, and is usually according to negative criteria. People are screened out because they have the wrong qualifications for the job, no previous experience or other justifiable reasons. Reasons for screening out must be justifiable, or rejected applicants may seek redress in law if their rejection was unfair. This applies at any stage of the selection process, and unsuccessful candidates may ask for the reasons for not being selected.

Weighted application blanks (WABs)

While standard application forms give a great deal of information in an orderly manner, each one needs careful scrutiny. If a large number of applications is received, this can be very time-consuming and expensive to screen, if a manager's time is involved. WABs are application forms which are highly structured, so that answers can be scored differentially for different jobs. These can be scored by a clerical worker, and the highest-scoring applicants put forward for further selection procedures.

Criteria measures are used for critical dimensions of the job. For example, if a degree in Psychology is essential to the job and all applicants appear to have some experience, the criteria measure may be set as 'at least an Upper Second Class Honours degree in Psychology'.

Biographical inventories (BIBs)

These forms enquire into an applicant's past, on the assumption that past predicts future performance. This assumption may not be true; people sometimes need a change of environment in order to become motivated, or demotivated. It is difficult to enquire about areas such as motivation on application forms; this may be discussed at interview, which is usually the procedure which follows screened applications.

Drakeley (1989) suggested that the selection of questions for biodata forms follows directly from the job analysis. Questions usually take the form of multiple choice, in order to score them objectively. Again, this can be done by a clerical officer. Scores may be listed on the same summary sheet as any other data, giving an overall picture of the applicant.

This type of questionnaire could, in fact, replace the letter of application if letter-writing skills are not necessarily part of the job, as literacy is assumed from graduate or graduate equivalents. There may be some inaccuracies arising from memory lapses and distortions on the part of the applicant. In addition, information may be distorted if applicants leave out details or magnify items which they feel would stand them in good stead. Even weighted forms cannot compensate for this.

Objectively scored biodata may produce a pattern which has been found to be useful for predicting performance of future applicants. Owens and Schoenfeldt (1979) suggested that individuals with similar patterns of input and prior experience variables will behave in a similar way and can be subgrouped on this basis.

A weighted questionnaire with 263 items was tested on office staff and was found to correlate with job performance and length of stay within the organisation. Reilly and Chao (1982) reviewed a number of studies investigating the use of biodata and found it to be one of the three best indicators of entry level job performance, with a validity only bettered by ability tests and job tryouts. There seems every reason to sustain the inclusion of weighted application forms in the selection procedures, with added job-related questions and clerical profiling of replies, to save management time.

Job tasks and job tryouts

Applicants may be invited to an organisation for a job tryout, which is an informal way for the applicant and the organisation to assess whether they belong together. Job tasks may form part of a number of formalised selection procedures, often taking one or two days in all. The job tasks consist of a set portion of the actual job, and are observed and assessed by someone from the organisation, often a Line Manager. Job tasks give a measure of current performance rather than past performance, which is indicated on application forms or reference reports. Reilly and Chao (op. cit.) found these to be a good predictor of job performance. In addition to being useful for the organisation, it is informative for the applicant and carries high face validity as far as the applicant is concerned (face validity means that on the surface it appears to be testing what is being sought).

Interviews

These may be **structured**, where set questions will be asked of all applicants so that their replies can be compared more easily. This would seem to be a fair process, except that special strengths of some individuals may be overlooked. This can be rectified in part by asking at the end of the set questions whether the applicant has anything to add in support of their application.

Unstructured interviews are those which have no set questions, but interviewer and interviewee set the parameters as they go along. This can bring out the strengths of the applicant, although a reticent applicant may not perform well. In addition, it is more difficult to make comparisons between applicants, as different topics may have been covered.

It would appear that many organisations place a great deal of weighting on the interview, yet, as Herriott (1989) suggests, 'most interviews are poor selection tools'. He advocates the structured interview, where researchers have, in some situations, found validity to be higher (e.g. Latham and Saari, 1984, selection of foremen). In unstructured interviews, validity was found to be lower than other selection methods in a review of a number of studies carried out (Hunter and Hunter, 1984), and reliability is far below the level acceptable for a psychometric test (Reilly and Chao, 1982).

Stereotypes and interviewer bias

Reilly and Chao's study also indicates bias in interview situations. Women tend to be discriminated against, especially in applications for managerial posts, presumably because managerial roles are seen to require 'masculine' characteristics. Interviewers may identify traits and assess them correctly in applicants, but these may not really be essential to the job, only in the eyes of that interviewer. If a panel of interviewers is used and they fail to agree on the right applicant for the job, this shows low inter-rater reliability[1]. The criteria were not clearly defined in advance so that they each knew what they were looking for in an applicant.

Kinicki and Lockwood (1985) suggest that the suitability of the interviewee would be predicted by various factors, one of which was whether he or she was the same gender as the interviewer. In order to avoid allegations of bias, it might be advisable to have equal numbers of male and female interviewers on the panel.

Since we tend to like those who are like ourselves, attraction to an interviewee (Wanous, 1980) can result in organisational cloning. Organisations can also keep their personality by attracting people like those selecting them, and by attrition (Schneider, 1987).

It should also be remembered that interviews are processes which are open to impression management. However, interviews fulfil a role by allowing both parties to clarify what each expects of the other. Selection is a reciprocal decision-making process – interviews allow an individual to assess the organisation, as well as the organisation to assess the individual.

Reference reports

It is common practice to ask for a reference from an individual's previous or current employer, or, if previous experience of the job is unnecessary, a character reference from a professional person who knows the individual well.

References may be structured or unstructured. **Unstructured** references give the referee the opportunity to say what they see as important about the applicant. This may not be what the new organisation needs to know. In addition, bad points can be omitted. **Structured** references take the form of specific questions which have to be answered or boxes which have to be ticked (see Figure 2.1). A form is sent to referees nominated by the applicant, one of whom is usually the current employer, if employed. These pro-forma contain specific questions, primarily about observable behaviour or extra-curricular

[1] *Inter-rater reliability*: the amount of agreement between raters; high levels of agreement indicate a reliable judgement has been made.

activities thought likely to predict success in the job. Sometimes verification of biodata is requested, for example, length of employment, work status, salary level. Referees are asked to tick appropriate response boxes in reply to each question: these may be ranked from good to bad. Counterbalancing may be used, so that 'good' is not always in the same column (boxes are not, of course, labelled good/bad, but the regularity of the format may make this obvious).

Referees may also be invited to send letters if they wish to add anything which is not covered on the form. Responses may be checked by telephone or questioned further, especially if there appear to be omissions or discrepancies.

Dobson (1989) states that structured references have been shown to be preferable to unstructured ones, giving the referee guidance as to what behaviours are relevant, and causing a referee to re-evaluate his or her own judgements. However Cronbach (1955) found that, when rating scales are used to measure impressions of personality, judges use different scales – some are more lenient than others. This prompted the comment that possibly references tell us more about the referee than the candidate!

Even structured references are open to enhancement by an employer who wishes to rid himself or herself of an unwanted employee. This may be one of the causes of people being promoted above the level of their capabilities. Perhaps this could be obviated by obtaining a reference from their penultimate employer.

Please tick the appropriate box for each question:

	Good	Moderate	Bad
1. How would you describe the applicant's timekeeping?			
2. How would you describe the applicant's attendance record?			

FIGURE 2.1 *Sample questions from a reference report form*

Reference reports seem a cost-effective method of obtaining information or verifying information given by a candidate (Beason and Belt, 1976; Nash and Carroll, 1970). Surprisingly enough, few studies have been carried out on the reliability of reports: Mosel and Goheen (1982) investigated the level of agreement between referees for an applicant and found it to be high, whereas in 1959, they had found that references given by supervisors produced only a low correlation with those give by acquaintances. Validity studies, e.g. Hunter and Hunter's meta-analysis[1] (1984), Reilly and Chao (1982) and Cascio (1978), found reference reports produced low correlations with many criteria, including performance, tenure and training success, which would appear to suggest that references should not be the main course of staff selection, but used as a form of verification, bearing in mind that views expressed in references are still somewhat subjective.

Psychometric tests

Psychometric tests are usually regarded as being more objective than other methods of personnel selection, because they are less subject to bias on the part of the employer than interviews, and less able to misrepresent the applicant than reference reports or inaccurate application forms and letters. It is useful to have some objective measures of applicants' abilities, not only for selection purposes, but in order to refute any claims by unsuccessful candidates that they were treated unfairly; employers must be ready to defend their decisions as to why candidates have not been appointed.

There are a number of different types of psychometric tests used in selection procedures: cognitive tests, personality tests, intelligence tests, aptitude tests, skills tests and simulated job-task tests. Tests which are relevant to the job are chosen for inclusion in the personnel selection process; careful selection of tests is essential. Test publishers supply reliability and validity coefficients for each test, together with norms for specific populations; these are too many and varied to be discussed here.

Types of test

1 **Cognitive tests**. Investigate perceptual abilities, memory tasks and may involve forms of verbal reasoning.
2 **Intelligence tests**. May form a baseline criterion for a job, that is applicants have to score above a certain level in order to proceed to the next selection procedure. These tests do not usually relate directly to a specific job.
3 **Aptitude tests**. Investigate whether people have an aptitude for a type of job, even if they have never done it before. For example, they might be

[1]Meta-analysis is a process of analysing data from a number of studies on the same topic. As these studies were undertaken with different populations, at different times, statistical adjustment is necessary in order that the results are meaningful.

given tests of manual dexterity if they are applying for jobs assembling circuit boards.

4 **Skills tests**. Specific skills are tested to establish the exact level of an applicant's skill in relation to other applicants. Previous employers may all have rated their employees as having 'good' skills, but what is good to one may only be average to another. An independent assessment draws finer comparisons.

5 **Job-task tests**. May not be exactly the same as the tasks to be performed on the job, but may be similar, in order to assess potential capabilities, but avoid measuring badly trained job practices.

6 **Personality tests**. Personality may not be seen as relevant to all jobs (perhaps mistakenly so). Increasingly, personality tests are being used for managerial level appointments, as the personality of the manager is frequently seen to be linked with effective management. However it must be remembered that most personality tests were originally designed to identify those with personality problems; using these one would not expect high validity in an occupational setting. Occupational tests for managerial qualities have now been specifically designed.

In order to be effective, psychometric tests must be fair.

Non-UK nationals may be disadvantaged, especially if (a) English is their second language, or (b) their culture is very different from that of the UK.

If some applicants are from within the organisation while others are external applicants, psychometric tests show everyone that they are being treated the same, especially if these are used as a screening process before interview. Applicants who do badly on the tests can be screened out and sent home, thereby pre-empting questions concerning the subjectivity of the interview situation.

Box 2.2 Assessment centres

Assessment centres are run independently of organisations, but are used by them when selecting personnel (usually for management-level posts) or for identifying existing personnel who would be potential managers.

As a rule, candidates attend the centres for more than one day and undertake a series of tests. These may include psychometric tests, job tasks, interviews and other assessment activities, such as leaderless discussion groups. Candidates are observed and their performances scored. At the end of the assessment, selection decisions can be made. The process is seen as unbiased and objective, although some investigators still question inter-rater reliability.

SUMMARY

Any organisation is likely to want the 'best' employees it can find. Job analysis is the first step, to establish what the job entails. Recruitment follows and then appropriate selection processes. These may include application forms, interviews, job tests, psychometric tests, references. Usually several selection techniques are used for verification. The techniques selected may depend on the type of job as well as the organisation concerned. Assessment centres may be used, usually for managerial positions, but also for choices for internal promotion or employee development.

chapter three

MOTIVATION IN THE WORKPLACE

CHAPTER OVERVIEW

This chapter aims to provide a working definition of motivation and discuss its importance to the individual and the organisation. Some theories of motivation are described and their relevance to the workplace is evaluated in terms of how they can be applied to enrich jobs, increase job satisfaction and improve productivity.

INTRODUCTION: DEFINING MOTIVATION

What causes people to behave as they do? In fact, what causes them to do anything at all? These questions underpin psychologists' investigations into motivation, which has been a central topic for some decades now. When we consider work, which many people profess to dislike as a global concept, if not their own specific job, then why do they do it? According to Steers and Porter (1983), motivation is the force that:

1 energises (causes people to act)
2 directs behaviour (towards specific goals)
3 sustains behaviour (until goals are achieved).

This definition implies that motivation is a sustained state, rather than a flash-in-the-pan event. As far as work is concerned, one can hope this is so. Once the individual is energised, work behaviour is directed, possibly by others or by external forces as well as internal preferences, and sustained until the job is done, or until the work day finishes.

But what motivates people to work in the first place? Is it money and material gains (Taylor, 1916)? Or is it the need for interpersonal interactions (Mayo, 1933)? Is it a need to feel needed, or a need to feel powerful? Or an interaction of all these factors – and more? If Taylor's theory was the whole answer, no-one would take up certain jobs, such as nursing, which involves unsocial hours, sometimes unpleasant work and is not very highly paid.

Two extreme theories of motivation were outlined by McGregor (1957) (see Box 3.1). Theory X represented the traditional view of management, McGregor said, while Theory Y was the position industry should aim to encourage – self-reliance rather than being directed by the big stick. The truth probably lies somewhere between the two positions, but neither explains *why* people take up either of these two positions, or perhaps more important, why they should move from one to the other.

Box 3.1 McGregor's Theory X and Theory Y

Theory X states that:

- Workers inherently dislike work.
- Workers must be coerced and controlled.
- The average worker shuns responsibility.
- Workers have little ambition to grow in the job.
- Workers are not interested in organisational goals.

Theory Y states that:

- Workers find work as a natural part of their lives.
- Workers are self-motivated.
- Workers desire responsibility.
- Workers are committed to organisational goals.

If increased motivation leads to increased work and increased output, then insight into what the motivators are is obviously going to be useful to industry and commerce. There are many theories of work motivation; in order to provide a theoretical framework, we have linked some of these into broad categories with common theoretical underpinnings. The three categories selected are: reinforcement theories, need theories and cognitive theories.

REINFORCEMENT THEORIES

1 Taylor: Scientific Management

Taylor (1916) was one of the first people to look into what motivates people at work. He proposed what was called Scientific Management, the goal of which was to reduce fatigue associated with the job and to pay fair wages. Taylor believed that the worker was motivated by money as reward, but tiring job tasks reduced productivity.

Taylor's suggestion that workers were motivated by money was accepted without question. His observations on worker fatigue reducing productivity, however, prompted research into job design, to try to improve physical conditions at work.

Taylor also proposed, but never tested, the concept that work satisfaction was related to productivity. From the 1930s onwards, the concept of job satisfaction became all-important, in an attempt to explain why some people would perform badly paid, seemingly difficult jobs. It was suggested that they gained a form of inner satisfaction from the job itself, an intrinsic reward. Research into job satisfaction and productivity is inconclusive; some studies find a relationship, others do not.

2 Skinner: reinforcement theory

Skinner (1938) proposed that behaviours which are rewarded will be repeated. He used the term 'reinforced' rather than rewarded, because he believed that 'rewards' are specific to the individual at any one time. **Positive reinforcement** is a form of reward which the individual finds pleasant. In the workplace, this is usually praise, approval or money. Punishment is an unpleasant occurrence following a behaviour; this is likely to deter the behaviour in future. In the workplace, this could be a strong reprimand from a manager. **Negative reinforcement** is when unpleasant circumstances occur, but are removed following a specific behaviour. For example, I may have no money to buy food, therefore I am hungry; if I wash dishes at the restaurant, they will give me a meal. According to Skinner, the most powerful form of reinforcement is positive reinforcement.

Schedules of reinforcement were investigated in studies with animals. When reinforcement is not given for every response, it is called partial reinforcement, and this is available on a number of different schedules:

1 **Fixed ratio:** one reinforcement is given for a set number of responses. This yields a fast response rate.
2 **Fixed interval:** one reinforcement is given after a fixed interval of time, provided at least one response has been made. This yields a medium response rate.
3 **Variable ratio:** one reinforcement is given *on average* for a number of responses. This yields a fast response rate.
4 **Variable interval:** one reinforcement is given after variable intervals of time, provided one response has been made. This also yields a fast response rate.

If money is the reinforcer in the workplace, there would be difficulty in applying variable interval schedules, as people need to know when they are to be paid. However, adaptations of these schedules are used, in the form of bonus schemes or forms of reinforcement other than money.

Skinner did not research his theory in the workplace, but the concept of reinforcement has been utilised in the workplace by others, notably Hamner.

3 Clay Hamner: reinforcement theory and contingency management

One of the main criticisms of Skinner's theory is that it does not account for how behaviour occurs originally, in order for it to be reinforced. In the workplace, Hamner (1974) suggests that behaviour is learned by first-hand observation; this enables the behaviour to be reproduced and subsequently rewarded. This follows the pattern of operant conditioning suggested by Skinner, where voluntary responses are made in order to obtain reinforcement. In applying reinforcement theory to the workplace, Hamner suggests a number of managerial actions. Contingencies should be arranged in order to produce the desired behaviours in the workplace. If fixed-schedule reinforcement is used, it may appear to the worker that he or she is being reinforced for poor performance, if there is a time lag between the reinforceable behaviour and the reinforcement. This highlights one of the problems in the workplace: immediate reinforcement for good performance is not always available; even praise may not always be practicable immediately following appropriate behaviour, unless managers are constantly on hand.

Hamner suggests that bonus schemes are effective positive reinforcers. Principles of **avoidance learning** can be utilised in some circumstances; for example, getting to work on time avoids loss of pay. These methods strengthen desired workplace behaviours. Undesirable behaviours may be weakened by either punishment or by the principle of **extinction of behaviours**. Punishment may take the form of severe reprimands or loss of pay. Principles of extinction are the non-rewarding or ignoring of bad behaviours. In the workplace, this could take the form of not being paid for substandard work. The idea of 'payment by results' has recently been under discussion in a number of work areas, including education. The variety of 'raw materials' (i.e. students!) would seem to make this an unfair proposal, which could raise even more problems in the workplace. In industry, the raw materials supplied to two different factory sites may differ, causing unfair comparisons to be made. This could be demotivating for workers.

Hamner suggested a set of rules for managers when applying operant conditioning techniques.

1 Don't reward everyone the same; we all need to feel different and need to have an achievable goal to aim for.
2 Remember that a manager's behaviour either reinforces or does not reinforce workers' behaviours. Managers are never 'neutral'.
3 Tell your workforce what will be reinforced.
4 Tell them what they are doing right or doing wrong. In other words, give

feedback.

5 Don't punish in front of others. This involves loss of 'face' for the worker, which builds resentment and is demotivating.
6 Make the consequences of workers' actions equal the behaviour.

Many theories of motivation include elements of reinforcement theory. The problem which remains is, which reinforcements are appropriate, and for which workers?

4 Herzberg's two-factor theory

If we take the wider view of reinforcement as being individually determined (what reinforces one person does not necessarily reinforce another), we can include Herzberg's theory as a reinforcement theory. It also introduces the concept of job dissatisfaction, which has the opposite effect from motivation, and could possibly be viewed as non-reinforcement, if not a form of punishment.

Herzberg carried out a survey in 1959 with groups of engineers and accountants to find out what employees found motivating at work, what made them feel good or bad about their jobs. On analysis, he found that replies fell into two clusters or **factors**. One factor was associated with job satisfaction, which he called a **motivator**, and the other was associated with dissatisfaction – this he called the **hygiene factor** (see Box 3.2).

Box 3.2 Hertzberg's motivators and hygiene factors

Motivators	**Hygiene factors**
Achievement	Working conditions
Recognition	Type of supervision
Responsibility	Relationships with co-workers
Opportunity for advancement	Company policies
Interesting work	Pay

To keep workers happy and motivated, Herzberg suggested, job dissatisfaction must be eliminated by providing basic hygiene factors. In addition, motivators to improve performance must be present.

Subsequent research failed to identify the same two factors (Schneider and Locke, 1971). Dunnette et al. (1967) suggested the theory is only applicable to white-collar workers, but a recent study would seem to indicate the division is not as simplistic as white- or blue-collar workers.[1]

[1]The term *white-collar workers* refers to clerical or managerial staff; *blue-collar workers* refers to more manual occupations.

Kohjasten (1993) looked at motivation in managers in the private and public sectors, using Herzberg's model. Pay and job security were found to be greater motivators for private-sector managers than public-sector managers (viewed as hygiene factors by Herzberg). Recognition for work achievements were greater motivators for public-sector managers. There may be other variables involved in the division of factors, for example personality, which influences job choices as well as being subject to the influence of motivational factors.

The main value of Herzberg's theory is that it has stimulated strategies to improve job interest for employees, such as job enrichment programmes and job rotation (described in more detail in Job Attitudes and Job Design from pages 15–17). Programmes giving workers more responsibility have met with mixed results; motivation and work performance have not always increased. Possibly not everyone regards increased responsibility as reinforcement, even though they may pay lip-service to it. Some people may feel that resposibility or new job titles should be matched by increased pay; hygiene factors have to change too, or dissatisfaction will outweigh any increase in job satisfaction.

Evaluation of reinforcement theories

If we understand 'reinforcement' in the sense of money and material gains, as Taylor suggested, then the theory does not hold for all jobs – or conversely, we should all want the same job, the one that pays the best! On the other hand, if we adopt Skinner's view, that 'reinforcement' means different things to different individuals, we have a wider view of jobs and their reinforcers – what is reinforcement to one person is not necessarily so to another. This can account for why we do not all chose the same jobs, we are not all looking for the same reinforcers. However, even this seems simplistic when we try to account for the differential effects of modifying reinforcement on individuals in the same jobs. Other factors seem to be involved besides simple cause and effect.

NEED THEORIES

A number of theories of motivation suggest that people have needs which are satisfied by working. These may be tangible, such as the need for food or money to pay the rent. Less tangible but equally real needs include social contact and interaction, or a need for respect from others.

1 Maslow's need hierachy theory

Maslow (1970) suggested that we have a hierachy of needs (see Figure 3.1 opposite).

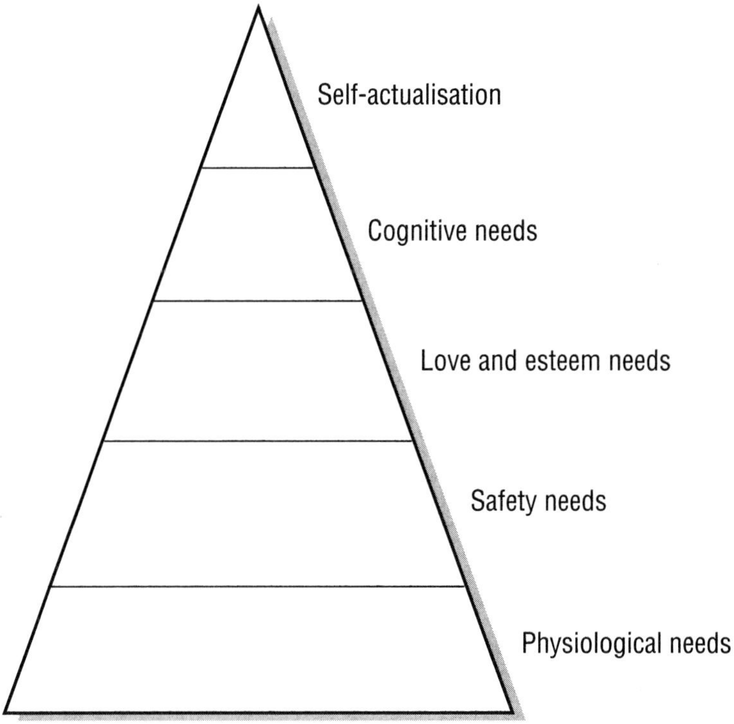

FIGURE 3.1 *Maslow's need hierarchy theory*

Our basic physiological needs for food and drink have to be satisfied before we feel the next tier of needs, shelter and safety. Fulfilment of these needs leads us to look for social needs such as friendship, followed by esteem needs, to have our accomplishments recognised by our peers. Self-actualisation is the achievement of one's highest potential; whether this is ever achieved is a point for discussion. If we reach our pinnacle, are we then demotivated, as there is nothing left to strive for?

Maslow's theory seems to fit the work situation quite happily, although the upper tiers may not apply to everyone in the workforce. There is always a higher tier to strive for, as once a tier is achieved, it ceases to become a motivator. However, questions have been raised as to the sequence of the tiers, whether these are the same for everyone, and whether backward as well as forward movement is possible.

Research has not found much support for the theory (e.g. Rauschenberger et al., 1980). Application of the theory in order to motivate the workforce has likewise fallen short of expectations (Miner, 1983). The main asset of Maslow's theory is that it has humanistic appeal. It projects the idea that many human needs are bound up with work, not just the need for a pay cheque, as early theories suggested.

2 Alderfer's ERG theory

A variation on Maslow's theory is Alderfer's theory, where the tiers of Maslow's theory have been replaced by three types of needs.

1 Existence needs; these are physiological and safety needs.
2 'Relatedness' needs, which are met by social interactions.
3 Growth needs, for the individual to develop fully and achieve potential.

Alderfer does not insist that the needs are hierachical. An individual may use a lower-level need as a substitute if higher-level needs are frustrated. If, for example, you were unable to be promoted at work because there were no jobs available at a higher grade, although you knew that your work was of excellent quality, you might content yourself with a pay rise. This is at the level of Existence needs, and you are unlikely to boast of a pay rise to your co-workers, whereas promotion, which would be seen by everyone, would be at the level of Growth needs.

There has been little research into ERG theory. Like Maslow's theory, it is very general and best viewed as explanatory or descriptive, rather than predictive of how motivation can be improved in the workplace.

3 McClelland's achievement-motivation theory

Unlike the two theories previously described in this section, McClelland's theory was developed specifically for work motivation. McClelland suggested that people are motivated by different patterns of needs, drawn from three key areas.

1 **Need for achievement**: the desire to get the job done, to solve problems, face challenges.
2 **Need for power**: status-oriented people who need to have influence, wish to control others or reach a prestigious appointment, rather than solve problems or achieve goals.
3 **Need for affiliation**: the need to be liked and accepted. They are motivated by co-operative work situations rather than competitive ones and are very concerned with interpersonal relationships.

According to McClelland, we all possess all of these needs, though in an individual combination; generally, one need is predominant. Most research on this theory has focused on the need for achievement (McClelland, 1961). It has been suggested that people who have a high need for achievement do best in jobs which require problem-solving abilities. People with a high need for power should thrive in jobs where they can be in charge. McClelland and Boyatzis (1982) gave questionnaires concerning achievement needs to managers and potential managers, and found a high positive correlation between managerial positions and the need for power. Those with a high need for affiliation do best in a team-working situation.

A direct application of this theory is to improve workers' motivation by matching each individual's need profile with job requirements, so that each person can fulfil his or her predominant needs.

Evaluation of need theories

Need theories have an intuitive appeal, probably because we like to feel that work satisfies an inner need other than greed or love of money, and also because they view people as different individuals, not just 'workers'. These theories have been instrumental in setting up useful intervention strategies (Miner, 1983), matching individuals' jobs to fulfilling their individual needs. This idea of fitting the job to the person, rather than fitting the person to the job, has far-reaching implications for job design and evaluation. This concept underpins much of the current thinking in Human Resource planning; whether it will be found to be impracticable or too expensive remains to be seen.

Cognitive Theories

These are theories which give heed to the worker as a rational, thinking being who will weigh up the pros and cons of the work situation in order to decide where individual rewards and gratifications lie, putting motivation on an individual basis. Extended theories suggest that employers provide a range of potential rewards and allow employees to chose their own reward pattern.

1 Equity theory

You may already be familiar with the Social Psychology theory of Social Exchange, where people weigh up what an action will cost them against the benefits it will confer, in order to estimate the overall reward. Adams (1965) applied this to the workplace, where the 'costs' of working (tiredness, inconvenience, lack of free time, etc.) are weighed against the benefits (salary, socialisation, etc.). Adams suggests that employees have to feel that the exchange is 'fair' in order to feel motivated to produce a good work performance.

Equity theory has been extended and has now become quite a popular theory. It suggests that workers bring certain inputs to the job in terms of, for example, energy, effort, qualifications. These may be either **perceived** (Ip), open to the employees' subjective assessment, or **actual** (Ia). In return, workers expect certain outcomes, such as pay, recognition, job involvement and fringe benefits, and again these may be either perceived (Op) or actual

(Oa). Workers make comparisons with others in similar posts, to ascertain the equity of their own position. Equity can be expressed as: $\frac{Op}{Ip} = \frac{Oa}{Ia}$

Inequity can be perceived by the worker in one of two directions, both of which may reduce motivation. **Underpayment inequity** results when a worker feels that outcomes are too few for the inputs he or she is making, compared to others.

Imagine you have been working for a company for some time, and because they are expanding, they take on another person to do the same job as yourself. This is someone younger than you, with less experience, no company 'years' to credit, yet you find out this person is actually paid £5 per week more than you. What would you do? You could decide to try to rebalance your situation by doing one of the following:

1 **Increase outcomes**: ask for a raise or find other 'perks' from your job.
2 **Decrease inputs**: limit your work production or be less careful about quality.
3 **Change the comparison other**: decide the individual in question was an unfair comparison for you, a new 'whiz kid' with whom you could not possibly compete, whereas Old Fred, who has worked for the company for as many years as you, is on the same pay as yourself.
4 **Distort inputs/outcomes**: argue to yourself that perhaps you are not working as well as you thought, or that you do not need any more money to live on (this may sound like another theory, Cognitive Dissonance.)
5 **Leaving the situation:** decide that the inequity of your work situation forces you to leave.

Now imagine that you are the new employee in this scenario: how would you feel about being in an **overpayment equity** situation? This, too, creates an imbalance, according to the theory. You may decide to:

1 **Increase inputs**: work harder.
2 **Decrease outcomes**: ask for a pay cut – not very likely!
3 **Change the comparison others**: use the rationale that obviously you are an interim grade, probably being groomed for stardom.
4 **Distort inputs/outcomes**: my work is of a very high quality, I am worth every penny I am paid.

Although Equity Theory has been researched a great deal, most early studies were laboratory based. A field study was undertaken of attitudes of 2,000 workers to a two-tier pay structure in a retail industry, where new employees were taken on at a lower pay-scale. The lower-paid workers, who were recently employed, perceived inequity in pay, because they compared themselves to higher-paid workers, who were doing the same kind of job. The higher-paid workers, however, did not perceive inequity (overpayment of themselves), because they were drawing comparisons to the pay structure before the two-tier system was introduced. This study confirmed the predictions of Equity theory, in both underpayment and overpayment equity situations (Martin and Peterson, 1987). These results would seem to indicate that a two-tier pay structure would reduce motivation among the workforce.

In a study of 764 African-American workers, Perry (1993) found that both types of inequity showed effects, as predicted by Equity Theory, on self-reported job-related skills and job satisfaction. Workers chose a self-protective strategy in either case. A survey evaluating income distribution in industry also showed findings consistent with Equity Theory (van Wijck, 1994).

However, very little application of Equity Theory in the workplace has ensued. Other variables, such as individuals' sensitivity to inequity, may need identification and further research before useful applications can be made.

2 VIE theory of motivation

Sometimes referred to as Expectancy Theory, the basic tenets were introduced by Vroom (1964). Later refinements have been added by other researchers. There are three components to VIE theory.

1 **Valence**
How much the outcome is worth to the individual. This is a subjective evaluation, because not all outcomes mean the same to all workers. Some are interested in working to achieve a bonus, some for promotion, some to avoid the supervisor's displeasure and some merely to keep their heads above water. As we said in connection with reinforcement theories, we do not all have the same reinforcers. (VIE Theory is sometimes called a reinforcement theory, but the rationalisation carried out by individuals, according to this theory, puts it into the cognitive category.)
2 **Expectancy**
There are two areas of expectancy, both of which involve subjective estimation. The worker assesses how much effort he or she needs to expend in order to complete the work, and also what the probability is that the work can be completed successfully.
3 **Instrumentality**
The expectation of what the outcome will be if the work behaviour is performed. An individual may work hard in order to achieve the desired outcome of promotion and/or a pay rise. The probability of a pay rise may be high, as recognition for hard work, but the probability of promotion may be low, as it may be contingent on a superior retiring or beating other applicants to the job. Other variables may well intervene; if this is perceived to be so, motivation may break down.

VIE Theory allows for the fact that motivation is complex, involving a number of factors, and also highly subjective. People have highly individual forms of rationalisation, which on analysis, may not be logical to others. It looks at the relationship between effort and performance, performance and outcomes, and how desired those outcomes are to individuals. Studies using the VIE model of work motivation have supported the theory and highlighted practical suggestions for improving work motivation, by clearly defining outcomes and performance-related goals. Mastrofski et al. (1994) found the concepts of VIE Theory consistent with the results of their work with police officers, relating to 'arrest productivity' (the number of arrests made by officers). Feather (1992) found that Equity Theory was directly applicable to job-seeking behaviour among unemployed people studied.

3 Goal-setting theory

This theory is usually attributed to Locke (1968), although goal-setting programmes had been used in industry well before that date. Locke investigated the idea in order to provide specific parameters. The basic concept is that workers can be motivated to achieve a specific stated goal. By assigning a specific task, it implies that it is finite, whereas simply urging people to 'work harder' has little or no effect. Goals can be seen to be achievable, whereas work stretching to infinity can be demoralising. Goal-setting is sometimes referred to as a reinforcement theory, but as workers are often asked to assign their own goals, this would involve cognitive functioning.

Laboratory and field research support goal-setting as a motivator. A field experiment was set up involving 209 engineers, divided into three experimental groups and three control groups. All the experimental groups were set goals, whereas the control groups had no set goals. The groups were studied over a period of nine months. The 'goals' groups were superior to the 'no-goals' groups in terms of cost control, quality control and intrinsic satisfaction. (Ivancevich and McMahon, 1982).

Goal-setting is a process frequently used in organisations, often inducing healthy competition between departments or individuals, provided this is not explicitly promoted by managers. The following guidelines have been found to be useful:

1. Set goals should be challenging but obtainable (Erez and Zidon, 1984).
2. Goal commitment should be obtained from workers (Locke et al., 1981).
3. Support elements should be provided. (It is no use asking for increased production if you then run out of raw materials. Encouragement, moral support and support staff are also essential.)
4. Pressure to achieve goals should not be used as it may result in expediency or dishonesty.
5. Providing feedback *en route* to the goal sustains and increases motivation (Locke, op. cit.).
6. Goals set by workers themselves provide increased motivation (Erez and Arad, 1986).

Goal-setting is a useful theory which can be applied in a wide range of work settings, at all levels, and in other fields; sports psychology in particular has adopted its recommendations. Weinberg's (1978) critique of Locke's model in a sport and exercise setting found strong relationships between goal difficulty and performance achieved. The concept of goal-setting has been incorporated into a number of incentive programmes and management by objectives (MBO) techniques in a number of work areas.

Evaluation of cognitive theories of motivation

Cognitive theories of motivation view motivation as being mediated by the individual's thought processes, although there is no real proof that this is always so. Distortions, such as those used in rebalancing an individual's inputs/outcomes in Equity Theory, weaken the predictive power of rational theories – because people often act irrationally. Goal-setting directs an individual's thought processes and focuses the attention, thereby providing a vehicle for motivation. It is, however, more of a technique than a complete theory of motivation.

Box 3.3 Job attitudes, job design and job satisfaction

Early theories of motivation indicated job satisfaction as an intangible element of reward. The concept was used to describe why individuals chose occupations which were demanding, either physically or psychologically, yet provided few tangible rewards. Herzberg later linked the concept of job dissatisfaction with areas which, if they were inadequate, became demotivators.

These polarities became the basis of trying to assess people's job attitudes. This included more than simply liking or disliking the job, but encompassed how much job involvement people felt. If they were actively and emotionally involved with their jobs, it was argued, they were likely to feel a greater degree of organisational commitment. This describes the extent to which people identify with and are involved with an organisation.

Methods were sought which would make jobs more agreeable, consequently increasing motivation and organisational commitment. Job enrichment involves redesigning jobs to give employees a role in planning, executing and evaluating their work. Job rotation is used to prevent boredom in repetitive task areas. Workers are trained in several jobs and rotate through these, spending a specific amount of time at each. Job enlargement is where an employee is allowed to take on extra tasks, if they wish. This needs to be handled carefully, as it can be construed as 'doing more work for the same pay', likewise job enrichment, which we mentioned previously, where employees are encouraged to take additional responsibility.

As with other methods of attempting to increase motivation, there are as many claims of failure for these methods as there are claims for success. A direct relationship between job satisfaction and job performance (output or productivity) would seem to be obvious, yet research studies show a low correlation between those two variables. Lawler and Porter (1967) suggest that the relationship is not a direct one, as we might expect, but complex, influenced by many personal and situational variables.

OVERVIEW OF MOTIVATION AT WORK

So, how is an employer to motivate the workforce? Which is the best technique to use? Which is the best theory? The short answer is that we still do not know. Techniques and applied theories which increase motivation and productivity in one situation are not necessarily successful in another. Individual and situational variables encompass such a wide range that no single ruling is available. Perhaps it is necessary to apply something of *all* the theories to increase worker motivation. This seemed to be the view of Steers and Porter (1979), who wrote:

> 'Individuals who have particularly strong needs (e.g. need for achievement) may also be inclined to make equity comparisons with regard to how their peers are being rewarded in relation to the types and amounts of rewards that they themselves are receiving. Not only that, but they will likely be sensitive to what it is that they do that results in "good" responses – and thus will likely form ideas (i.e. expectancies) that a certain action (behaviour) on their part will, or will not, result in a "good response" (i.e. reward) next time.'
>
> (*Motivation and Work Behaviour*, 2nd edition)

SUMMARY

Theories of motivation have developed over the years, using principles of reinforcement theory, need theories and cognitive theories. These have been applied to job design, in attempts to broaden the scope and enjoyment of work, besides providing tangible rewards, such as pay. As yet, no single, infallible method of increasing worker motivation has been identified.

chapter four

LEADERSHIP, GROUPS AND GROUP PROCESSES

CHAPTER OVERVIEW

Most, if not all, organisations have a leader, and sections within that organisation may have other leaders. Groups within the organisation may be structured or unstructured, but all have a function to perform. The processes assisting those groups to function will be examined, with special attention paid to communication, how groups make decisions and why this process can go wrong.

LEADERSHIP

One area of organisational life where psychology has contributed distinctive understanding is that of leadership and, by direct implication, work groups, for while there may be (at least notionally) groups without leaders, it is impossible to have leaders without groups.

One definition of leadership suggests that it is the ability to lead a group towards the achievement of its goals. However, leadership is not a unitary phenomenon; there are many facets to be considered. Is the leader to be elected or imposed? What are the functions to be performed (for example, which power is relevant to the leader, the group and the situation in hand?). French and Raven (1959) identified five main bases of power:

1 **Reward power**: the leader has the power to give rewards. If followers value those rewards, they will respond to the leader. If the leader has no contol over rewards they value, then the leader is perceived to have no reward power.
2 **Expert power**: superior knowledge and expertise in the relevant tasks confers the right to lead upon the leader.
3 **Coercive power**: followers believe that the leader is able to administer penalties which they do not want to incur. These may take the form of loss of pay, verbal abuse, withdrawal of support (although since the 1974 Employment Act, workers are protected against summary dismissal).

4 **Referent power**: followers believe that the leader has characteristics that are desirable and that they would wish to emulate.
5 **Legitimate power**: sometimes called 'position power', it relies on followers believing that authority is vested in the leader and that he or she has the right to give orders.

One leader may operate from more than one power base. The leader may have expert power, referent power and reward power, for example. All these power bases, however, rest upon the beliefs of the followers, to a greater or lesser degree.

In examining the social psychology of organisations, Katz and Kahn (1978) suggest that true leadership obtains more than mechanical compliance. A leader is necessary to interpret organisational rules, indicate boundaries, change environmental conditions, encourage positive interaction and provide continuity in an organisation. However, Kerr and Jermier (1978) suggest that where subordinates exhibit the need for independence, indifference to organisational rewards, a professional orientation and closely knit, cohesive work groups, leadership will be neutralised and rendered ineffective. From these two views, the organisation can choose its best approach. In an organisation where all staff are professionals with a high need for autonomy, expensive middle management is largely unnecessary, whereas in an industrial situation, using a number of semi-skilled staff employed in tasks which may change periodically, a careful choice of leaders will ensure maximum value to the organisation.

It should be clarified that there is a difference between supervision and executive leadership, as indicated by Hollander and Offerman (1990). Executive leadership is concerned with the ability to affect large number of followers, rather than only immediate subordinates. Early research tended to ignore the distinction between these two types of leadership, which may account for some apparently conflicting results, but with hindsight, it is often possible to allocate studies to one or other area.

Trait Theories

Early theories of leadership which were trait-centred (called the 'Great Man approach', leaving us in no doubt as to the perceived gender of leaders!) were probably testing for attributes of executive leadership. The idea which was current at the time suggested that leaders possessed characteristics and traits in common; these were the basic attributes of leaders. The fact that some research studies were inconclusive may have been due to the inclusion of data from supervisory leaders. Stogdill (1974) reviewed and summarised trait studies and listed desirable leadership characteristics, such as a desire for responsibility and task completion, self-confidence, tolerance of frustration.

However, these traits are not very helpful in identifying future leaders in advance, as they become evident during the course of leadership.

BEHAVIOURAL THEORIES

Having failed to isolate a range of characteristics displayed by leaders, researchers turned their attention to behaviours, to see if it was possible to identify specific behaviours common to most leaders. A number of surveys, of both leaders and their subordinates, enquired into leadership behaviour. From the responses to an industrial study looking at leaders in industry, Likert (1961) found that two main behavioural styles were indicated. Displaying **task-oriented behaviours**, leaders concentrated on getting the job done. Leaders whose behaviours were **relationship-oriented**, concentrated more on maintaining social relationships within the workplace. These, Likert (1967) suggested, were more effective and had lower staff turnover rates. These findings reflect those of Halpin and Winer (1957), who called the leaders' behaviours (a) **initiating structure** and (b) **consideration**.

This has direct application in organisations where project managers are appointed on a rotating basis, with different people fulfilling the leadership role for various stages of the project life cycle, dependent upon the demands of the situation at any one time. The manager who plans and manages the project may well need different characteristics from the manager who performs the sweeping-up operations, recording lessons learned from that project in order to be readily available for future work. While the former may need dynamism, entrepreneurial skills and proven ability in the field, the latter would need an ability to pay attention to detail and to analyse intelligently. Psychometric tests could be useful in identifying appropriate personnel and in fact, Halpin and Winer's concepts of Structure and Consideration form the basis of a test called The Leadership Opinion Questionnaire (see Figure 4.1 overleaf), which can be used to identify an individual's potential leadership style. These concepts appear as separate dimensions, independent of each other. It is possible for an individual to score high on both, low on both or differently on each.

The classic study of Lewin, Lippitt and White (1939) found that autocratic leadership styles increased productivity but did not lead to good social interaction patterns within work groups, whereas democratic leadership improved both, and **laissez-faire** leadership (leaving people to their own devices, not displaying any form of leadership) reduced both. Vroom and Mann (1960) suggested that the apparent superiority of democratic leadership is no longer in evidence, if the main criteria is task accomplishment. Rosenbaum and Rosenbaum (1971) found that productivity is increased when autocratic leadership is used in situations which are highly stressful to employees in some way. Using this model, organisations might chose a leader to improve productivity or interpersonal relationships, as appropriate. However, introducing a leader with a totally different syle may be counter-productive, if the work force object. Leaders need their groups behind them.

How often do you: *Please tick appropriate box*

	Always	Often	Sometimes	Seldom	Never
1. Put the welfare of the unit above the welfare of any person in it?					
2. Give in to your subordinates in discussions with them?					
3. Encourage after-duty work by persons in your unit?					

FIGURE 4.1 *Extract from the Leadership Opinion Questionnaire. (Fleischman, E.A. Reproduced by permission of the test publisher. Copyright © 1989 McGraw-Hill/London House, a division of the McGraw-Hill Companies, Inc)*

Contingency Theories

Subsequent contingency theories proposed that appropriate leadership behaviour is **contingent** (or hinges) upon characteristics of the leader, the situation and the subordinates (as mentioned earlier, leaders are inextricably involved with groups!).

1 Fiedler's contingency model (1967)

This suggested that good leadership performance from a task-oriented leader occurs in situations giving high and low situational control, whereas relationship-oriented leaders give optimum performance in situations involving moderate control (see Box 4.1).

A review of the predictive ability of this model showed support in half of the laboratory studies, but rather less in the field studies (Peters et al.,1985). The

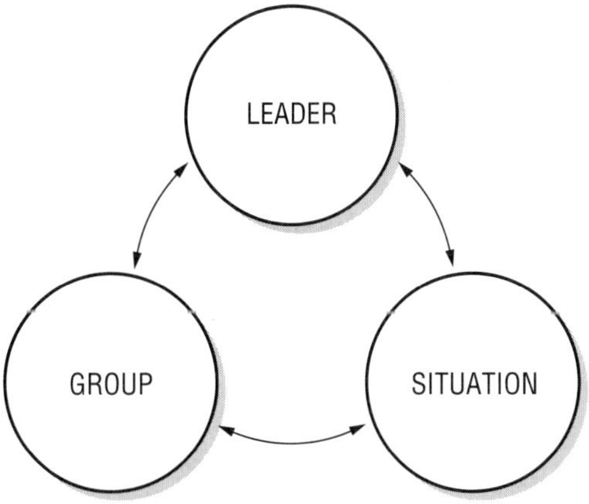

FIGURE 4.2 *Contingency models of leadership*

authors suggest that, to apply the model in the workplace, other variables would need to be included. This highlights one of the other major criticisms of Fiedler's theory, that it takes an overly simplistic view of the work setting, where so many interacting variables occur. The other main criticism concerns the measure his theory uses, LPC. No one really knows exactly what it is that LPC measures. Is it a measure of the leader's ability to relate to other people, rather than a work-related characteristic?

Box 4.1 Predicted Effective Leadership (according to Fiedler's Contingency Model)

From replies to Fiedler's questionnaire about the leader's Least Preferred Co-worker (LPC), a score is obtained relating to that leader's style of leadership; this is regarded as a fixed trait by this model.

Given other variables, such as task structure, leader's power position and group/leader attitudes, the most effective leader can be predicted as either task-oriented or relationship-oriented. For example:

Group/leader attitudes	Task structure	Power position	Predicted effective leader
good	structured	high	task
good	structured	low	task
poor	structured	high	relationship
poor	unstructured	high	relationship
poor	unstructured	low	task

In the last example, it has been found that, given all the negative circumstances, the leader's best action is to 'get on with the task'!

2 House's path-goal model of leadership (1971)

This is closely tied to general expectancy theory of work motivation, as described in the previous chapter. As such, it can be assumed to indicate strategies which would be useful if directly applied in the organisational setting. Performance goals are set by leaders and paths are provided for the subordinate, who may then achieve appropriate reward goals. The leader must know what rewards each subordinate desires, and in satisfying those, the subordinate finds the leader's behaviour acceptable.

In a review of forty-eight studies, involving nearly 12,000 participants, reasonable support was found for the model, in most areas (Indvik, 1986). Specific goal-setting has been shown to be a potent motivator and improver of performance by both experimental and field studies. The path-goal model is explanatory, rather than predictive, as is Fiedler's theory.

Where next?

Current research is once again refocused on leadership traits, in an effort to enhance leadership in organisations, in order to improve productivity, efficiency and competitiveness. This time, emphasis is on what Hollander and Offerman (1990) called 'executive leadership'. An important trait is thought to be charisma (charm, magnetism, appeal).

Transformational leadership

Tichy and Devanna (1986) suggest the term 'transformational leadership' to denote the leader who recognises the need for organisational change, has the ability to plan for it, the courage to implement it and the charisma to take others with him or her. A formal examination of 'charisma' is emphasised by Conger and Kanungo (1987) to delineate the behavioural differences of charismatic and non-charismatic leaders. House, Spangler and Woycke (1989 working paper) linked the notions of charisma and transformational leadership in a study to understand the success of American Presidents, as rated by experts. This idea would seem to be encouraged by Bower and Weinberg (1988) who advise top managers to think of their organisations as miniature states or economies, and practise statecraft.

Women as leaders

Early studies of women as managers and leaders suggested that women lacked self-confidence, feared success, had been socialised into not wanting leadership roles, were more people-oriented than task-oriented – in fact, producing the 'female stereotype'. Later studies aimed to look at the difference between male and female managers in terms of characteristics. This would seem to be a useful comparison, if we knew exactly which characteristics made a good manager! However, these studies are useful, in so far as they can demonstrate differences or similarities. In fact most indicated that male and female managers exhibit similar traits, according to self-reports and ratings by subordinates (Powell, 1988; Pfeffer and Shapiro, 1978; Watson, 1988). Statistics show that there are fewer women in leadership positions compared to the number of women in the workforce; an example of this is education, where the majority of teachers are women, but only between four and ten per cent of headteachers are women.

In Northern Ireland, Cromie (1981) sent questionnaires to male and female teachers, managers and secretaries, enquiring into factors such as job involvement, job commitment and competence. Replies indicated that women felt as much job commitment as men; women felt that they could do management type jobs as competently as men, but men felt that women were less competent. It would appear that discrimination may play a large part in keeping women out of leadership especially as new managers are appointed by other (higher) managers, who are probably men!

Training leaders

A leader's personal traits are important, not only because they fulfil the expectations and stereotype of 'what a leader is like', but because they also affect the reciprocal relationship with those who are to be led – the inevitable leader-plus-group interaction. Organisational psychologists can help train future leaders to understand these interactions and relationships, as well as assisting the selection of potential leaders for given situations in the first place. In a survey carried out by The Industrial Society (1985; reported by Sadler, 1989), ninety-seven per cent of companies responding said that they trained their managers, while only sixty-two per cent trained manual workers.

A range of techniques is used in management training, from laboratory-based activities to outdoor activities (as described in Chapter 7). Many of these are still being evaluated; no one method has been identified as 'best'.

Groups and group processes

A group may be briefly defined as two or more people with shared goals. Within an organisation, there may be formal and informal groups; although only formal groups may be set up by the organisation, frequently informal groups are equally important to its members.

Formal groups

Formal groups may be permanent groups, such as a sales team or a manufacturing unit, which always work together. Some formal groups are formed on a temporary basis as a task force for a specific project or length of time. Members of these groups may also be members of other formal groups, such as unions or committees, and also belong to informal groups as well. Formal groups are structured and task-oriented.

Informal groups

Informal groups may be friendship groups or groups which form because they have shared interests or simply happen to take break-times together. The importance of these social contacts is not to be underestimated – as we saw from the chapter on motivation, people do not simply go to work for money, but often for the social interaction which work brings. In fact, these social networks may often be maintaining a work system which is not perceived by the management. For example, informal work groups had formed among the cleaning staff at a hospital, where they had made friendships on their particular ward, arranged coffee and lunch breaks together and networked a social system. An Organisation and Methods team reorganised the cleaning of the hospital on a pooled-resource basis, so that staff no longer worked in the same place each day with the same people, with the aim of covering absences and holidays more efficiently. What they found happened was that absenteeism rose and staff began to leave. 'Efficiency' had disrupted the harmonious workings of a social system which was perceived as highly important to its members. When the 'old' system was reinstated, harmony and efficiency were regained. (From Huczynski and Fitzpatrick, *Managing Employee Absence for a Competitive Edge*. Pitman: London, 1989, pp 44–6.)

ROLES

Within groups, individuals usually adopt or are assigned roles. This may be on the basis of expertise or other characteristics which the individual displays. As the group begins to function, these roles may become more defined; this is a process known as **role differentiation**. Some groups may not be assigned a leader, sometimes an individual will take on a leadership role, through aspects of seniority or expert knowledge.

Experimental work by Bales and Slater (1955) showed that even in newly formed groups, leaders emerged. Using Bales' Interaction Process Analysis

(1950), they identified both task leaders and socio-emotional leaders. These were never one and the same individual, but fulfilled different leadership roles. Task leaders were oriented towards the end product of the job task; socio-emotional leaders looked after the social and emotional needs of the group, which often helped keep the group functioning harmoniously. Task orientation and relationship orientation, as we saw earlier, had been identified in a number of studies on leadership, and appear without prompting in group studies. Bales did not find these two roles occurring in one and the same person, yet in assigned leadership, one person is expected to fulfil both roles. Role conflict may occur in individuals who have more than one role, perhaps in two different groups, which may seem to be serving two different goals; this may result in stress for the individual concerned.

GROUP NORMS

Norms are the unwritten rules that groups adhere to, in order to function. There may be norms for group productivity – people will be 'discouraged' from working too fast or too slow, thereby offending the group norm. There may be a dress-code norm, of formal or informal clothes, or norms of behaviour, such as how much input each person gives in group discussions. Norms may give group members a feeling of cohesiveness and shared identity. Feldman (1984) suggests that norms may come about in a number of ways. There may be explicit instruction from existing group members to a new member, or implicit agreement, for example, that some work practices have produced poor results in the past and will not be used again. Socialisation also produces norms, for example, in some workplaces, work may not begin for the first twenty minutes, while everyone has a cup of coffee.

GROUP PROCESSES

Group processes describe the way in which groups function. They look at the interactions which take place (group dynamics) and the communications routes in use, all of which make use of group norms and shared beliefs. These are intragroup processes, processes which go on within any one group.

Conformity

Group norms are adhered to through conformity. Actions which violate group norms will be dealt with by the group. Through conformity the group continues to function as a group, rather than a collection of individuals.

Cohesiveness

The closeness and attraction between group members may have a strong influence on productivity and the quality of work produced by the group. This may be due to 'team spirit' and not wanting to let other team members down, also wanting to be valued by other members of the group who are valued in return. Group cohesiveness is increased by all members having equal status in the group. Similarity of characteristics and stability of group members also have positive influence on cohesion. Smaller groups are usually more cohesive; their members have greater opportunity to interact with each of the other group members, which increases the 'we-ness' feeling. The presence of an external threat also increases group cohesion, identified as 'in-group/out-group' concepts by Tajfel et al. (1971). Competition with other groups is a factor in enhancing group identity.

Competition and co-operation

Work groups are formed with the purpose of achieving organisational goals, and may also serve personal needs. Co-operation is expected among members of the same work group; co-operation is often necessary between groups (inter-group process), in order to achieve a goal; for example, the flight crew of an aircraft rely heavily on the ground crew, in order to be able to perform their job tasks.

Competition is most frequently a between-groups process, where groups aim to outshine other work teams. Sometimes competition occurs within a group, as with a sales team; they are considered as a group, but each individual competes in order to be 'salesperson of the month'. In this event, competition is encouraged, as inter-group competition frequently is. Occasionally competition can become a source of conflict.

Conflict

Conflict is behaviour which is designed to inhibit another from achieving set goals, either by a person or a group. Within an organisation, there are a number of forms of conflict:

- **intra-group conflict:** occurs between individuals of the same group, and interferes with the attainment of the group's goals
- **inter-group conflict:** conflict between two groups in an organisation, perhaps both bidding for the same resources
- **inter-individual conflict:** may arise as a dispute between two individuals in an organisation.

Sources of conflict

Conflicts may be caused by one or a number of different reasons. Scarce organisational resources, jealousy over status, disagreement between groups who rely on each other for their productivity, and perceived inequality, of pay or other benefits, may all lead to conflict. Perhaps the most usual form of conflict is management/worker conflict, possible because those involved may not perceive that they share the same goals. Management aims to increase productivity and cut costs; workers want to feel self-esteem and be paid well. This is an oversimplification, but illustrates that each group *perceives* the other to have different goals. Unfortunately, conflict can have adverse effects on the individual, in terms of stress, and on the organisation, in terms of productivity. Managing conflict is a skilled process; avoiding conflict is even more skilled. By finding shared common goals, conflict may be avoided or managed. One way of doing this is to involve both management and workers in decision-making processes. If resolution of a conflict seems impossible within an organisation, both sides may agree to go to arbitration. In the UK the arbitration body is ACAS, whose findings on any dispute must be accepted by both parties.

Box 4.2 Quality Circles

This is a group of employees who meet to discuss work problems. The aim of the group meeting is to maintain or improve the quality of work. Employees become involved in work decisions and put forward ideas of their own. Quality Circles were originally proposed in America, but are most frequently utilised by Japanese management. Research into the efficacy of Quality Circles seems to suggest that most are effective initially, but lose their effectiveness after a few years. (Perhaps due to the Hawthorne Effect.)

COMMUNICATIONS

Communications may be at **macro-level**, between the organisation and the environment, or **micro-level**, between groups or individuals within the organisation. These may be verbal or non-verbal. Macro-level would include advertising, sales force, exhibitions, public relations and any other presentations to competitors or the world at large. Micro-level would include the formal and informal communications networks within an organisation.

Informal networks are often referred to as the 'grapevine'. This frequently operates between members of informal groups, although it may also serve formal groups. Information passed this way is often surprisingly accurate, although frequently disparaged as being just 'hearsay'. Formal communications may take a number of different formats within an organisation, both verbal and written.

The communications process

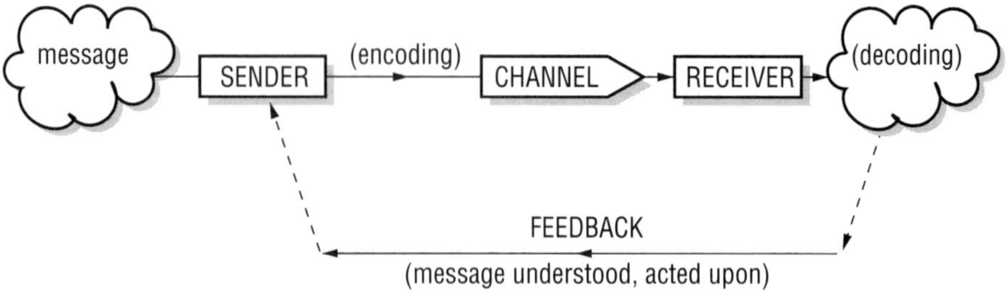

FIGURE 4.3 *The communications process*

The sender of a message chooses the appropriate channel for the message and encodes it appropriately. Written messages tend to have deeper coding than verbal messages; for example, over the desk, a sales manager may say 'Invite that chap from Bloggs Limited out for a drink', whereas in writing he might state: 'Continued interface with this section of the potential market is desirable'. Messages are decoded by the recipient, who needs the ability to decode messages, act upon the message and give feedback to the sender that the message has been received and understood. Encoding often uses jargon which may be specific to that organisation or industry, and therefore difficult for 'outsiders' to understand. New employees have to learn the appropriate jargon, in order to encode and decode efficiently.

Channels of communication

Communications may be sent through an organisation in one of the following ways:

- **top-down**: information, especially about decisions, is often disseminated from higher management levels, through middle management, to the main workforce
- **bottom-up**: information, possibly about workforce or machinery problems, is sent upwards through levels of the organisation
- **laterally**: information or requests may be sent across a strata of the organisation, where it is seen as relevant to that level only.

Verbal communications may take the form of:

- **Meetings**
  Advantages here include input from more than one individual and the spreading of information to a number of people at the same time, thereby saving time and effort. Problems which may arise include the possibility of one person dominating the meeting, to the exclusion of other potentially good inputs and participants not all 'hearing' the same message.
- **Personal contact**
  In a face-to-face situation, individual problems can be sorted out, information given and feedback received immediately. Disadvantages include the necessity for spontaneous thinking and reacting, which some people find difficult. Also, the power or status of one participant may overule the other.
- **Telephone**
  This permits a two-way flow of information and gives immediate feedback. It is less personal than the face-to-face situation, as Milgram (1963) demonstrated in his studies on obedience; people find it easier to refuse over the telephone. There is also a greater possibility of misunderstanding, as non-verbal signals are not available to receivers. As humans, we understand a great deal of what is intended through facial expressions, body movements and gestures.
- **Teleconferencing**
  A recent innovation which is useful across distances. A group of individuals in one location have audio links (and sometimes visual links as well) with others from another location of the same organisation, or others in the same industry. Ideas can be exchanged and instant feedback given, and it is far cheaper than if all delegates had travelled to a central point to meet. However, the satisfaction of personal contact is lost; people do not always have the opportunity to speak when they would wish to do so, due to limited or complete lack of visual cues. In spite of these limitations, teleconferencing is likely to increase, as it saves a great deal of time and expense, and takes less organisation than a physical 'get-together'.

Written communications may be in the form of:

- **Letters**
  When circulated within an organisation, these give the message 'this is serious, take my message seriously'. These may be used to impart management decisions to departmental heads or the workforce.
- **Memos**
  These may simply request or impart information. They are usually brief and have the advantage over face-to-face communications in that there is a written record; however, feedback is slower.
- **Formal reports**
  These often serve to underline what has already been discussed in meetings, in order that there is no misunderstanding as to what has been agreed. Other reports may concern work projects or work practices. From

the report writer's point of view, advantages include being able to prepare the document in one's own time and circulate it widely. However, recipients may not all be able to decode it accurately. If it is lengthy, they may not be inclined to spare enough time to read it, so information may be lost.

Distortion

Distortion of messages may occur as they are passed on. You may have played the party game of 'Chinese Whispers', where a message is passed around a circle, whispered from one person to the next. The resultant message rarely bears any similarity to the one which started out. In organisations, the same thing can happen, either accidentally or on purpose. Distortion occurs where the information contained in the message is changed or altered in some way; this is more likely to occur where messages are passed verbally.

Filtering is a process whereby elements of a message are filtered out, because they are thought to be unnecessary or irrelevant to certain areas.

Censoring, on the other hand, is where elements are left out of a message so that certain areas or individuals may not be informed of items or events. Information about possible workforce redundancies or reductions, due to less work availability and the rising costs of labour, might be censored below management level to simply include information about rising costs and lower work availability.

Communication networks

Communication networks represent the systematic flow of information between individuals or departments within an organisation. These fall primarily into two categories, **centralised networks** and **decentralised networks** (see Figure 4.4 opposite).

Centralised

Centralised networks are those where the flow of information is in one direction, usually emanating from a group leader. These include the Chain, the Y and the Wheel (which may have more or less than the four 'spokes' shown in the diagram). The Y network is an inverted Y, where information from the 'top' is passed through a hierarchy to recipients for action. The Chain and the Y represent speedy modes of communication; the Wheel involves the sender in greater effort and receiving feedback from a number of different areas.

Decentralised

Decentralised networks are those such as the Circle and the All-channel routes, where information is spread through a number of individuals. These routes may be used by problem-solving teams or autonomous work groups (see Box 4.3, page 56) or the company's Board of Directors.

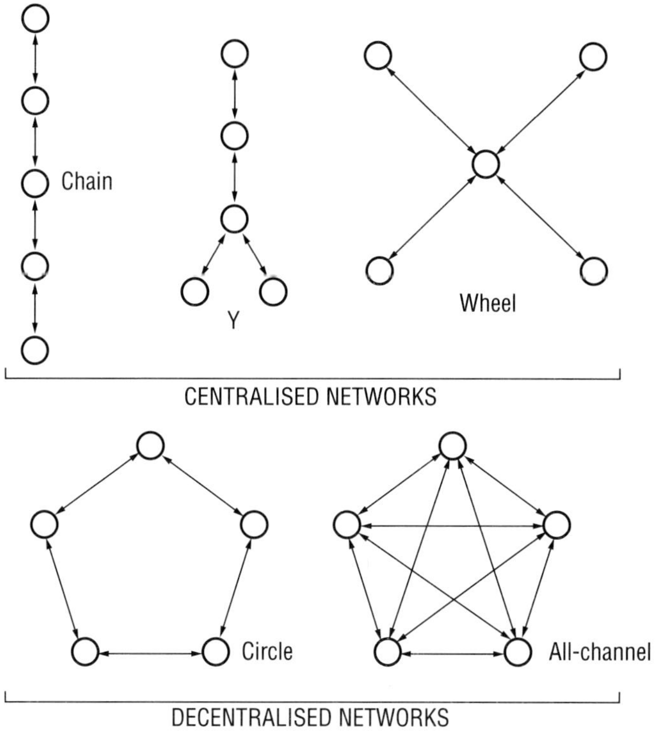

FIGURE 4.4 *Communications networks*

Most of the research on communications networks has been carried out in laboratories, which does leave us wondering how well this would generalise to the workplace (e.g. Shaw, 1954; Bavelas, 1950; Leavitt, 1951). These studies also indicated that different networks are associated with different levels of task satisfaction (although, again, these were laboratory tasks which had no real-life rewards or penalties attached). In centralised networks, satisfaction was low for all participants except the central member, whereas in decentralised networks, satifaction was equally high for all participants. This may have implications for job design in the real world, which was one reason why Volvo changed from line production to group work. A number of other organisations have done or are doing this. Interestingly enough, when Volvo last reorganised, they changed back to line work.

Box 4.3 Group working practices

In 1971, it was decided to change the Volvo car assembly plant in Kalmar, Sweden, from traditional line assembly processes to group work, in order to combat absenteeism and high staff turnover by increasing job satisfaction. Each team of fifteen to twenty-five members was given full responsibility for one component, such as upholstery, electrical system, etc., and assigned members to job tasks, set output rates, ordered supplies and inspected finished products. Absenteeism declined, turnover rates dropped and quality improved, although there was a slight drop in productivity. A few workers said they preferred the 'old' methods, but overall Volvo management declared the experiment a success and converted other production plants. Many companies have since followed suit, one recent example in the UK being Clarks shoe factories.

Team-building

When new work groups are formed, perhaps consisting of individuals who may not even know each other or have not worked together before, it is often necessary for team-building to take place. This may be informal or formal. Informal team-building, where individuals take a while to 'get to know' each other, has disadvantages in that one member may try to dominate the group, or reticent individuals may never get a chance to show their real skills. Formal team-building exercises may often be set up by organisations; these take place away from the work situation and usually contain activities which have little or no relationship to work skills. Individuals learn to work together as a group and value each other as individuals; strengths and weaknesses are recognised and understood. When the participants return to the work situation, they are ready to start work as a team.

Group decision-making processes

Effective communications channels are essential for effective functioning in organisations. Communication forms the basis of another essential organisational function, that of decision-making. Group processes for decision-making may be democratic, autocratic or by consensus.

Democratic decision-making process

This is a process whereby all members of the group discuss issues, and a decision is made with the agreement of all group members as to the course of action to be taken. Advantages are that there is input from a number of people, who may all have supplementary information or ideas, and that all members feel involved and are more likely to try to make the decision work. The disadvantage is that the process is time-consuming to allow for everyone to 'have their say'. In addition, the outcome may not be unanimous, but a case of 'majority rule', which could leave a disgruntled minority in some circumstances.

Autocratic decision-making process

This is where a decision is made by one person, usually the group leader, on the basis of information held by that individual alone. If that individual possesses all the information necessary for the decision, there may be no problem, but other individuals in the group may feel that they could have contributed further information and may be upset that they were not asked. If they do not agree with the decision, there may be further unrest. The main advantage of autocratic decision-making is that it is fast; occasionally in organisations, decisions must be made instantly – there is no time for consultation and discussion.

Consensus

This is a decision-making process which is based on agreement by every member of the group, without exception. As you can imagine, this can be an extremely time-consuming process, but one which may be necessary if, for example, the organisation is about to make radical changes. Juries are groups which are expected to reach consensus decisions because the outcome is so important – the freedom of an individual rests on their decision. In organisations, the decision may be equally important – people's jobs and livelihoods may rest on important organisational decisions.

Effectiveness of Group Decisions

In recent years, organisations have increased the amount of participative group decision-making. One reason is that a decision arrived at by a group commits that group to involvement, and work is likely to proceed more smoothly. In addition, group members can bring a number of areas of expertise to the discussion, and all facets can be examined in order to make the best possible decision.

But is a group decision better than one made by an individual? Research studies, by and large, tend to indicate that they are marginally better (Hill, 1982; Miner, 1984). Most of these studies are laboratory-based, as it is not often one gets the chance to compare the effects of two different decisions on the same problem in an organisational setting. However, group decision-making can become polarised, which results in groups coming to more extreme decisions than they would have as individuals.

'Risky-shift'

In 1961, Stoner carried out a series of experiments to compare individual with group decisions in areas which carried some risk associated with them. A typical problem he posed might be that a man was diagnosed as having a heart problem; should he change his active lifestyle or undergo heart surgery which might either cure him or prove fatal? He found that group members were willing to 'shift' from their individual tentative positions to a more risky decision once they became involved in group discussion.

Whether this would happen in real-life situations was a question which Janis (1972) decided to investigate by using retrospective studies (studies which look back on events). He chose to investigate group decisions which were later proved wrong. This does not indicate that *all* group decisions in real life are wrong – the 'right' ones slip by unnoticed!

Groupthink

Janis looked into the group decision-making processes which had brought about disastrous decisions for American Foreign Policy, such as the Bay of Pigs invasion in Cuba, the decision to cross the 38th Parallel in the Korean War and the decision to escalate the Vietnam War. He also investigated a number of industrial and commercial decisions which were failures.

He identified similarities in the processes of all of them, which he called Groupthink. The reasons behind Groupthink, he suggested, were:

1. Members of the group become so involved in the need to reach a unanimous decision that they fail to evaluate all alternatives.
2. The group sees itself as invulnerable. Faith in the group leads members to ignore the possibility of disaster following their decision.
3. Group members hold each other in high regard and censor any doubts they, themselves, may be thinking. The silence of dissent is mistaken for unanimity.
4. Direct pressure is applied to make group members conform.
5. The group shares beliefs and stereotypes, which leads to the suppression of negative information.

Janis also proposed that directive leaders generate Groupthink by discouraging other members' ideas. To avoid this, leaders should encourage discussion and criticism of as many ideas as possible.

SUMMARY

Current theories suggest that leaders in organisations have to take into account the types of groups which they lead, as well as the current organisational situation, in order to be seen as successful. Charisma is seen as a trait possessed by transformational leaders, who make real advances in their organisation. Work groups are set up for specific purposes and individuals define roles within those groups. Communications in organisations may be between individuals or organisational divisions. These communication channels may be used in group decision-making. Group leaders need to be aware of possible problems involved in group decisions, as these may not always be reliable if members insulate themselves from reality.

chapter five

HEALTH FACTORS IN ORGANISATIONS

CHAPTER OVERVIEW

This chapter introduces the basic ideas of ergonomics and how people interact with machines. It outlines some Health and Safety provisions for people at work and looks at the possible effects of poor working conditions and resultant occupational health problems, both physical and psychological.

ERGONOMICS

Ergonomics, or Human Factors as it is otherwise called, is an area where engineering and psychology interact. These may sound unlikely partners, but the users of machines are human, and have all the constraints of being human (see Box 5.1). These not only include the obvious physical ones of two arms and two legs, but also those constraints which are best known to psychologists, such as limited or selective attention, and other psychological limitations. Designers aim to cater for the 'majority' of the population, between the 5th and 95th percentile, or ninety per cent (see Figure 5.1 opposite), for any human attribute. Left-handed people will immediately take issue here – they account for approximately twenty per cent of the population, yet very few machines (even tin openers!) are designed for their use.

Box 5.1 Differences between human and machine characteristics

Human strengths	**Machine strengths**
Creative and adaptable	Makes few process errors
Can handle the unexpected	Does not fatigue
Uses information from many sources	Can store information efficiently (computers especially)
Corrects own mistakes	Can work in extreme heat, cold, wet, or radiation
Deals with ambiguity	Has high initial costs, but low long-term costs (maintenance)
Has low initial costs/ high long-term costs (wage increases, benefits)	

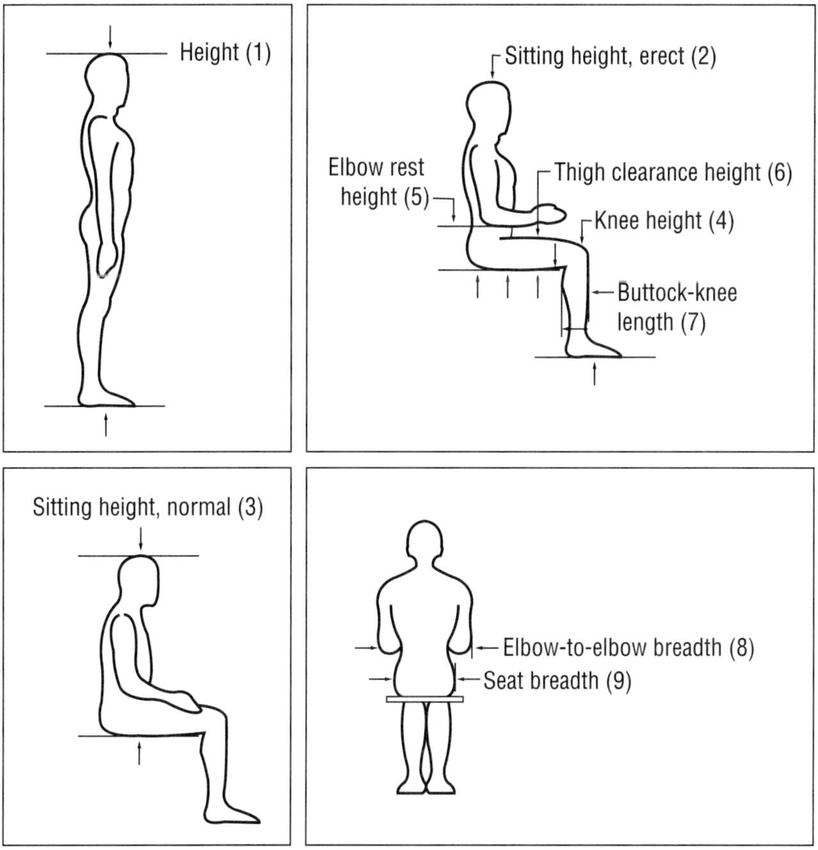

Selected structural body dimensions and weights of adults

Body feature	Dimension, inches						Dimension, cm*					
	Male, percentile			Female, percentile			Male, percentile			Female, percentile		
	5th	50th	95th	5th	50th	95th	5th	50th	95th	5th	50th	95th
1 Height	63.6	68.3	72.8	59.0	62.9	67.1	162	173	185	150	160	170
2 Sitting height, erect	33.2	35.7	38.0	30.9	33.4	35.7	84	91	97	79	85	91
3 Sitting height, normal	31.6	34.1	36.6	29.6	32.3	34.7	80	87	93	75	82	88
4 Knee height	19.3	21.4	23.4	17.9	19.6	21.5	49	54	59	46	50	55
5 Elbow-rest height	7.4	9.5	11.6	7.1	9.2	11.0	19	24	30	18	23	28
6 Thigh-clearance height	4.3	5.7	6.9	4.1	5.4	6.9	11	15	18	10	14	18
7 Buttock-knee length	21.3	23.3	25.2	20.4	22.4	24.5	54	59	64	52	57	63
8 Elbow-to-elbow breadth	13.7	16.5	19.9	12.3	15.1	19.3	35	42	51	31	38	49
9 Seat breadth	12.2	14.0	15.9	12.3	14.3	17.1	31	36	40	31	36	43
10 Weight†	120	166	217	104 lb	137	199	58	76	98	47 kg	62	90

†Weight give in pounds (first six columns) and kilograms (last six columns).
*Centimeter values rounded to whole numbers.

FIGURE 5.1 *Ergonomic data for humans from 5th to 95th percentile*

Human Factors specialists are involved in:

1. Planning work stations, so that personnel have everything within easy reach, and there is no constant crossing and re-crossing of tracks in order to perform job tasks.
2. Planning display panels, to ensure work information is easily accessible and comprehensible, by visual or auditory signals, with back-up signals for malfunctioning of critical equipment.
3. Planning systems, so that work moves in a logical series of processes towards an end product.

Thankfully, the days of the person having to fit the machine are over, and psychologists are tackling the person/system fit nowadays. Human factors need to be considered in designing systems, as well as machinery, in order to be user-centred. Ergonomics, engineering and systems design are combined in a bid to make the work environment more user-friendly. This has become particularly important since the introduction of computers in the workplace.

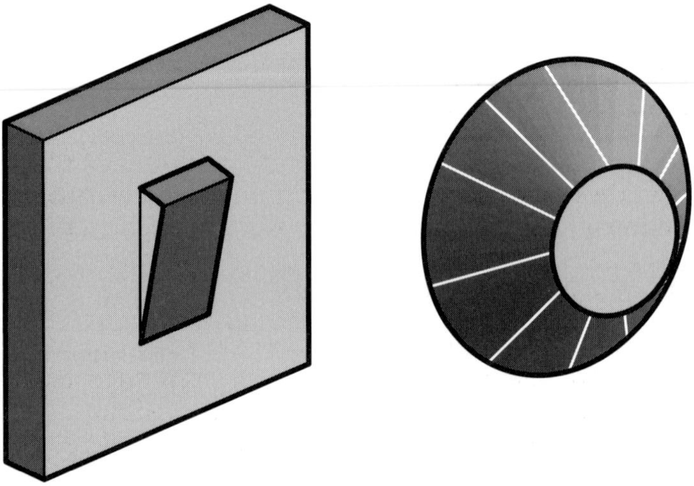

1. Is this light switch 'on' or 'off'?

2. Which way do you turn this control to switch the gas on?

FIGURE 5.2 *Switch Design. Switches should reflect the natural expectations and movements of the operators. If you turn a car steering wheel to the left, you expect the car to turn left. We 'expect' electric light switches to press down for 'on'. Labelling, colour coding and different shapes of switches may be necessary in a display panel containing a number of switches to avoid confusion*

Psychologists had to point out to employers that it was inhuman to expect an employee to sit before a computer for an eight-hour working day. Human Factors specialists propose the best ways for computer-dominated work environments to be managed, and are involved in designing work systems in other areas of industry and commerce, ensuring that the individual operator is considered from the start of the design process.

SYSTEMS

Any working process can be called a system, but the term is mainly used for a sequence of processes which has to be carried out in the direction of an end product (such as a manufacturing process). Some systems are almost fully automated, such as the car manufacturing companies which use robots for assembly and paint spraying. This avoids humans doing the heavy work and the health-hazardous work of spraying paint. People are in charge of the machines and are available for 'trouble-shooting'; others are needed for more complex tasks which the machines cannot undertake.

HUMAN LIMITATIONS

Human Factors specialists, while bearing in mind human physical limitations, are more concerned with psychological limitations. Not only whether they can see warning lights, but whether they will pay attention to them. And questions such as: How much information can one individual process at a given time? How long can they sustain attention?

Humans are fallible. They occasionally forget even the most important items (see Box 5.3), so fail-safe systems need to be incorporated into designs. Items such as warning lights are essential in case equipment malfunctions, with possibly an auditory warning as well, if the warning light goes unheeded for any length of time.

Vigilance

Display units, especially those which give warnings of breakdown or danger, must be clear and easily visible. Where operatives have to watch display units for signals, either to move on work tasks or to take emergency action, they need to be vigilant. Mackworth (1948) suggested that vigilance is decreased due to loss of sensitivity during sustained periods of attention. He carried out a number of experiments to test vigilance and performance decrement, including one where participants watched a radar screen for specific visual 'signals' against a background of visual 'noise'. They had to press a response button each time a signal was seen. Results showed that regular presentation of the signal, or signals in the centre of the display, increased detection rates; intermittent signals tended to be missed more often. Feedback to participants as to how well they were performing also tended to improve performance.

Wickens (1992) suggested that sustained attention in vigilance tasks is highly demanding of mental resources and therefore fatiguing. Where 'missed' signals are of crucial importance, for example air-traffic controllers at busy airports, frequent breaks should be taken to ensure a high level of performance whilst working.

THE WORK ENVIRONMENT

Factors in the physical work environment, such as noise, lighting, heating, the length of time a person works at a stretch, what time of day or night they work, may all contribute to the health and safety of the person at work. These factors may be crucial in defining whether accidents or illnesses occur as a result of work.

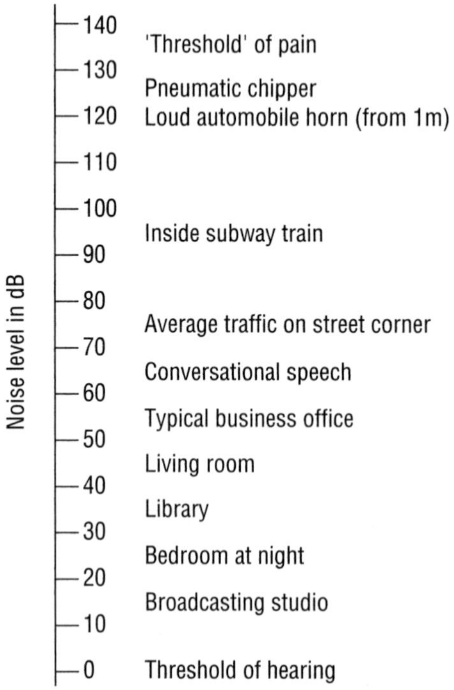

FIGURE 5.3 Some examples of common noise levels (in decibels – dB)

Noise

Very few people complain that their workplace is too quiet. Noise may be increased to the level where the listener suffers physical pain, due to the physiological mechanisms involved in hearing. Health and Safety legislation allows for an *average* daily personal noise level of 90 decibels (dB) (see Figure 5.3). If machinery noise exceeds this level, employees are only allowed to operate machinery for short periods of time, and must then be removed to a less noisy area. Machinery causing high noise levels often causes vibration, which can also be most unpleasant for the operative, road drills being an obvious example.

Psychologists have investigated the influence of noise in work situations (for a review, see Smith, 1995). Findings from research studies show that intermittent noise is more disruptive than continuous noise when both are at a reasonable level. Complex tasks, especially those requiring some thought, need a lower level of noise in order not to be disrupted.

Open-plan offices were designed to give the psychological advantage of breaking down social barriers which may occur in the workplace. However, these advantages do not always outweigh the disadvantages of loss of concentration which arises through increased noise and interruption. This problem can be resolved by increasing the amount of personal space per employee (resulting in fewer people in a large office) or reducing the overall size of the open-plan office, while maintaining personal space at the same level (fewer people in a small office) (see Figure 5.4 overleaf).

Noise in the workplace can often be reduced by insulation, machine housings and barriers between noisy machine areas. Vibration may be reduced by stabilisation methods. If a high level of noise is unavoidable for a greater part of the working day, ear protection should be provided and worn.

Lighting

The necessity for adequate lighting in order to perform the job task may seem an obvious requisite. If daylight is inadequate, it must be supplemented by artificial lighting. However, the optimal level of lighting depends on the task and the operative. Visual tasks involving small materials need more lighting, and older workers and others who spend most of the working day involved in visual tasks may need higher levels of lighting.

Conversely, glare can be a problem. This has been brought to the fore by computer operatives, where glare from their VDU screens was deemed responsible for headaches and eye problems. Glare-reducing screens are available now for VDUs; if light sources other than the VDU are reduced in intensity, this also benefits the operative. Glare reflected from shiny surfaces can also be a problem. Matt paint and work surfaces can counteract this, and

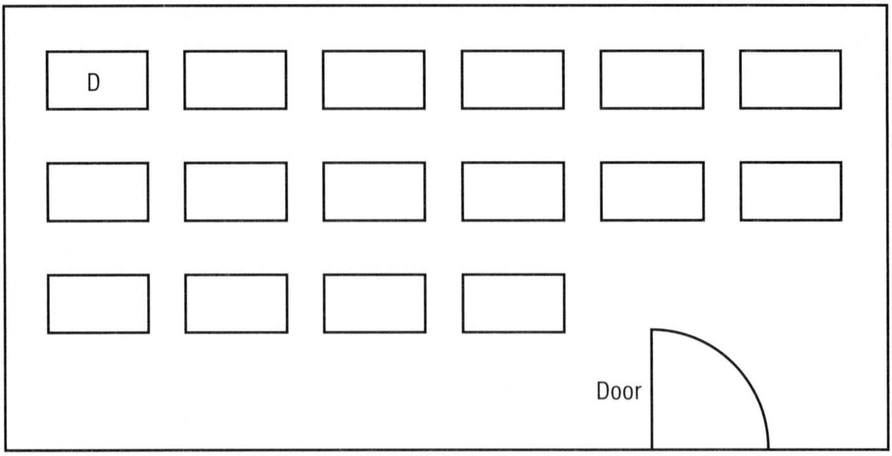

D = individual desk space

Open-plan offices adapted for better working.
In 1, an open-plan office makes for social equality, but is noisy, lacks privacy and is full of distractions. These large work spaces have mainly been replaced by adaptations, such as 2. Noise-absorbing, fabric-covered partitions (A in diagram) have been erected between work groups, while desk-height open counters (B in diagram) still maintain an open outlook into the rest of the room. Fitted carpets absorb noise, and plants and group-structured lighting provide a humanising effect. Workers report a greater feeling of privacy, less interruption of work through noise or distraction (Oldham 1988), while maintaining social equality and interactions with other members of the section. As desks can be placed directly against partitions, very little extra personal workspace is required.

2.

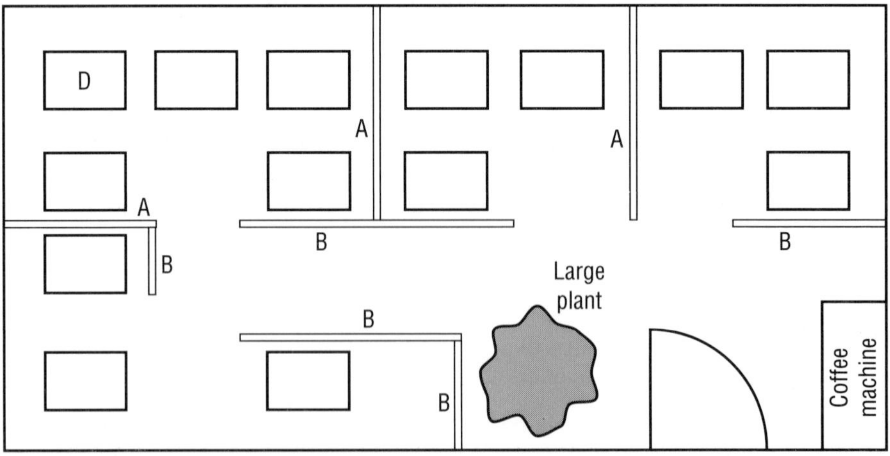

A = fabric-covered partition, 5' high
B = desk-height, counter-topped partition

FIGURE 5.4 Open-plan offices adapted for better working

metal machine surfaces can be crinkled rather than smooth, which reduces glare. Too much reflecting light can reduce the amount of detail which is observed, and flaws may not be detected so easily.

Heating

In the UK, workplaces must maintain a minimum temperature for reasons of employee comfort and efficiency. In offices, this is 60 degrees Fahrenheit. Outdoor workers have no such provision, but when temperatures fall too low, work is usually impossible because of ice or snow. Until the hot summer of 1995, few people realised that no upper-limit temperature exists in the UK, probably because there is not often need of one. Efficiency and comfort are likely to be greatly reduced by higher temperatures as well as low temperatures; current investigations suggest that stress levels may be increased in hot conditions.

Work times

Most full-time, paid work in the UK tends towards an eight-hour day (or night), during which time statutory breaks are to be taken. Separate legislation exists for specialised operatives such as coach or lorry drivers, where long spells of work could result in fatal accidents.

Compressed workweek

Some jobs have introduced a 'compressed' working week where three, four or five twelve-hour days are worked in succession, followed by a number of days off work, so that the overall working week is still maintained at about thirty-eight hours. On the whole, workers express a positive attitude to this, but some studies show that fatigue can be a problem, depending on the type of work. Data entry operators on a five-day twelve-hour schedule showed several signs of fatigue in that speed of response and accuracy decreased, which would seem to negate the organisation's aims of having a longer working day, as these were necessarily important attributes.

Flexitime

The introduction of flexitime, or flexible working hours, means that people can choose their hours of work, between set parameters, to fulfil a week's quota of hours. Studies on the efficacy of this have given varied results. In a review of these studies, Dunham et al. (1987) found there was no decrement in work performance, but there was no evidence of any increase either. However, absenteeism tended to decrease, as time did not have to be taken out of work time to get the car serviced, take children to the doctor's or fulfil other life tasks. In addition, there may be qualitative benefits which are not shown by the studies. For example, it may no longer be necessary to drive to work through rush-hour traffic, thereby reducing stress for some individuals; child care out of school hours may be distributed more easily between two parents working slightly different hours. It also gives the individual a feeling of control over some aspect of working life, which is also stress-reducing.

Shift work

A number of organisations use shift work, in order to keep functioning twenty-four hours a day; hospitals and other emergency services are obvious examples. Manufacturing industries which have expensive machinery do not want it lying idle for sixteen hours a day, so often organise workers around three eight-hour shifts. How does shift work affect the workforce?

The sleep/wake cycle is disturbed by rotating shifts; the circadian[1] rhythm is disrupted, and physiological mechanisms are out of alignment with the body's 'clock'. Eating at times which are unusual may cause digestive disorders and some workers report cardiovascular problems, according to a survey carried out by Wolinsky (1982). Night-shift workers are trying to work whilst their body clock is expecting to slow down to its lowest functioning; heart rate, breathing rate and blood pressure all drop significantly at night. Most studies show that people who work at night are less productive and make more errors (Gannon et al. 1983).

Box 5.2 Experiments with shift rotation

Czeisler *et al.* (1982) studied the work patterns and body rhythms of 130 shift workers at the Great Salt Lake Minerals and Chemicals Company. The company was operating three shifts around the clock, in a pattern of backwards rotation, that is to say, one week of nights followed by one week of late afternoons followed by one week of mornings. Czeisler's conclusions were that shifts should be rotated forwards (mornings then afternoons then nights), because the body's rhythms are more adaptable in a forwards direction. A weekly shift change is not beneficial either, as it takes almost a week for the body clock to adapt to the new schedule – maximum performance would therefore never be reached. A three-week schedule for each shift was recommended. The workers liked their new shift patterns; they adapted to them more easily, and their health improved. The organisation found that productivity improved significantly.

[1]*Circadian rhythm* is the name given to the body's daily pattern of sleeping, waking, eating, drinking, etc. It comes from the Latin *circa* meaning 'about' and *dies* meaning 'day'.

Health and Safety at work

The health of individuals at work is not just a matter for their own concern, but also, morally and legally, the concern of the organisation in which they work. Health and Safety legislation has increased over the years to provide employees with assurance of reasonable care and provision of safety on the part of their employers. If this is not provided and individuals are injured, either physically or mentally, then they have redress in law and may sue for compensation. In return, employees must take reasonable care of themselves and other co-workers.

The aim of the laws is the prevention of accidents and injury. Ergonomic data gives information on how people fit physically into their work environment, so that they are not working in a difficult position for long periods of time, which could result in deformation. Defining what standards are acceptable for mental health is more difficult, but progress in identifying these standards is being made, year by year. Stress resulting from organisational problems is a good case in point here. It has been recognised in law that, if stress results from an organisation's work practices, employees are entitled to recompense. Stress management programmes may be offered to employees to assist in dealing with stress, although ideally stress should be removed at source, rather than 'managed'.

Accidents at work are, statistically, less frequent than accidents in the home or car accidents, probably due to the large body of legislation in place to ensure workers' safety. The demographic group most likely to suffer accidents are young, male workers. Many reasons have been suggested: personality traits, inexperience with machinery, bravado about not taking safety precautions. When the YTS (Youth Training Scheme) was functioning, there was a high rate of accidents among the young people on the scheme, possibly for the above reasons, with the additional possibilities that they were not regarded as 'proper' employees by the organisation and therefore received less training and less care.

Are some people more prone to accidents than others, and if so, why? Statistically, alcoholics and drug takers have more accidents than most people, so alcoholism and drug addiction could be called predictors of accident-proneness. It is unlikely that these will be exhibited in the workplace, so are there other characteristics which could be predictors? The majority of studies have been carried out after car accidents, as these people are easily accessed. Fine (1963) surveyed 937 college students and found that the incidence of car accidents was significantly higher among the extroverts than among the introverts. This has subsequently been substantiated by many other studies. Other personality traits also found to be present in those involved in car accidents include: Type A behaviour, an external locus of control (both described later in this chapter) and neuroticism.

A comprehensive industrial study was carried out by Hansen (1989) with 362 workers in the chemical industry. Characteristics such as social maladjustment, various aspects of neurosis, cognitive abilities, employee age and length of service were examined to detect causal relationships involved in accidents. Results showed that some aspects of neurosis and social maladjustment are significantly related to accidents, even when allowances are made for age and level of risk exposure.

Furnham (1992) suggests that personality variables relate to all types of accidents and populations, accounting for about ten per cent of the variance. The two factors which seem to be the best predictors are a) extroversion/sensation-seeking/Type A behaviour, and b) neuroticism/anxiety/instability.

There are methodological problems with analysing work-related accidents. Accidents are reported as incidents, rather than processes; measures of exposure to the potentially hazardous situation are not included in the report. It is impossible to tell whether stress predisposed the worker to suffer the accident, or whether stress being suffered is the result of the accident, as investigations are necessarily *post hoc*. There are other confounding variables when

Box 5.3 How to turn a crisis into a near-disaster

Nuclear power stations use water in their cooling systems; if the reactors overheat, the end result could be a large radiation cloud spreading for miles around. The ensuing human tragedies which follow, as the world saw after the Chernobyl disaster, continue for decades.

In 1979, an employee at the Three Mile Island power station in the United States made a human error. He shut down an alternate feedwater pipe and forgot to turn it on again before he went off duty. This error was compounded by a design fault: there was no warning system to tell anyone else that the pipe was shut. A further equipment problem occurred in that the relief valve, which had been instructed to close, malfunctioned and remained open; however there was no warning to tell of this malfunction. The reactor began to overheat, warnings began to sound, and no one knew why. It took two hours eighteen minutes to diagnose the fault. In the meantime, the whole of the USA – especially local residents – began to panic.

Subsequent analysis showed up a number of design problems. For example, operators needed to scan 1,600 windows or gauges to detect faults in the system, and approximately 200 of these were flashing. Critical information was missing from the control panels some gauges were outside the work area and the same colours had different meanings (e.g. 'everything OK' and 'warning – problem') on different control panels used by the same operatives. The conclusions drawn were that, while human errors were involved, these resulted from grossly inadequate control-room design, procedures and training. Before 1979, no Human Factors experts were employed in the US nuclear power service; nowadays, they work in close collaboration.

making comparisons with car-driver accidents, for example. Workers who have had accidents may be moved to different work areas, or are unlikely to make the same error leading to the same type of accident again, whereas some car drivers never learn!

Occupational diseases

An occupational disease is one which is caused through an individual's occupation, but this is not always easily demonstrable. If an individual develops lung cancer, is it because of exposure to radiation in the uranium mine where the person works, or due to a lifelong habit of smoking? It is often difficult to pinpoint causes accurately, especially as many diseases do not manifest themselves for some time after exposure to the health hazard.

Historically, specific diseases were associated with specific areas of work, and there was little or nothing employees could do but grin and bear it. A historically important event was the 'Strike of the match girls' (!) in the nineteenth century, which highlighted industrial health problems. Workers in match factories used phosphorous, a substance known to have detrimental effects on health if not handled carefully. Workers in one factory formed themselves into a group and withdrew their labour from the factory until work practices were changed; this action was followed by workers in other factories.

Unions are often responsible for bringing pressure to bear on organisations to change work practices, once problems have been highlighted. Toxic chemicals are still a cause for concern today; as new chemicals are involved in industry, new problems are likely to come to light. Past problems include silicosis, suffered by coal miners who inhaled coal dust at the work face, and asbestosis, suffered by a number of workers in industries where asbestos was used as an insulation material and also by some demolition workers who were demolishing factories, machinery and buildings with a high asbestos content.

Repetitive strain injury (RSI) has been identified as a potential hazard for computer operators; this was one of the reasons why frequent breaks were deemed necessary for operators. Poor equipment and work-station design, combined with inadequate task design and work organisation, can cause disorders such as RSI or other limb disorders (Chaterjee, 1987, 1992). Work stations for VDU operators are now required by law to provide adequate space for movement and changes of position.

Prevention of occupational diseases is obviously better than cure. As hazards are identified, steps should be taken to protect employees who may come into contact with them. Physical hazards are far easier to identify than events which may cause psychological harm, such as traumatic events or psychological stressors.

Other workplace health problems

Many other problems can arise in the workplace which may be detrimental to the health of the employee and which may reduce productivity or cause accidents.

Substance abuse

The effects of alcohol or drug abuse may be found in the workplace, even if taken outside work premises. Many companies have strict and explicit rules about alcohol and drug taking; the penalty may be instant dismissal or disciplinary proceedings. The reasons for this are the work-related risk factors; operatives under the influence of drugs or alcohol are more likely to make cognitive or physical errors, which could result in accidents to themselves or other employees.

Mental health problems

Problems such as anxiety and depression, whether resulting from work or non-job causes, may have effects in the workplace. The chronically anxious person may have difficulty making decisions (Coleman et al., 1980); decision-making may be part of the job task and therefore essential to the organisation. Depression may result from chronic work overload or role conflict (Bromet et al., 1988); as such, it could be the organisation's responsibility to change work practices. Stress may be related to anxiety and depression; stress is such an important area of occupational health that we shall discuss this at greater length.

Summary

The use of ergonomic data tries to ensure that the workplace is designed to fit the individual. This way of thinking has now proceeded to designing job tasks and wider systems which are user-friendly. Many Health and Safety regulations have evolved from these findings. Organisations are legally bound to take reasonable care of their employees' health. The mental health of employees is also not to be endangered by poor work practices. Some organisations are taking positive steps to encourage good mental health among employees. These are seen to benefit both the individual and the organisation.

chapter six

STRESS AND ITS MANAGEMENT

CHAPTER OVERVIEW

This chapter enquires into the causes of stress, how it affects people, and what can be done about it. Some individuals appear to be more susceptible to stress than others and factors which have bearing on this are discussed. Stress can result from poor work practices or conditions. Models of stress are thus looked at in an organisational context, exploring some of the ways in which organisations can assist in stress reduction and stress management, by reorganising work practices to reduce stress at source, and by assisting individuals to manage their stress through programmes in the workplace.

INTRODUCTION: THE NATURE OF STRESS

There is no one definition of the term 'stress', yet we all seem to have some idea of what it constitutes. It may sometimes be defined as the physiological, psychological and emotional responses to threatening situations or events. This would seem to describe **acute stress**: a short period of time when something goes drastically wrong, when the individual's 'fight or flight' mechanisms are mobilised in order to deal with the problem, then all subsequently returns to normal. If, however, the problem persists, or the individual cannot deal with it, then **chronic stress** ensues.

There is the suggestion that a certain amount of stress is necessary for everyone in order to keep functioning. Some people may actively seek out stress, if their lives feel 'flat'. Psychologists have tried to distinguish between positive stress, which has been termed **eustress**, and detrimental stress, termed **distress**. The distinction is not clear-cut, because not everyone interprets the same events as positive or negative; stress is a personal issue.

Symptoms of stress can include:

- headaches

- knots of muscles in the back of the neck
- irritability for no apparent reason
- lack of concentration
- feelings of anxiety
- feeling depressed.

There are many other possibilities. These are subjective perceptions of stress which highlight some of your body's stress responses. There are also physiological responses occurring within your body of which you may be unaware, and you may also be adapting your behaviour in order to avoid or cope with your stressor (the things which cause you to feel stressed). These may well be different for everyone; what makes one person feel stressed may not affect everyone.

There are two important factors relating to stressors: their **controllability** and their **predictability**. Broadbent (1971) suggested that people who were able to predict when a noise was likely to occur found it less stressful than when the same noise level occured unpredictably. Stressors which we feel we can control are not perceived to be as threatening as those over which we can exert no control. Over the past ten years, more than 20,000 civil servants have been surveyed about their perceived sources of pressure at work, control over their work situation, health and health-related behaviours, such as smoking and drinking. Physiological measures were also taken; for example, electrocardiograms (to detect heart abnormalities) and blood samples, to determine levels of fibrinogen and cholesterol. High cholesterol levels have long been associated with coronary heart disease (CHD), so this was to serve as an indicator of those at risk. It was found that there was a strong relationship between high cholesterol levels and grades of employment, but not in the direction which you might expect. In fact, the highest cholesterol levels were found in the lowest employment grades, and the gradient declined until the lowest levels of cholesterol were found among the highest employment grades. The lower the grade of civil servant, the less control they reported having over their work and work-related decisions. The conclusion could be drawn that the lack of control was causing stress, indicated by the high cholesterol levels, which increased the risk of coronary heart disease (Brunner et al., 1993).

If an individual's stressor occurs in the work situation, it is encountered on a daily basis, and there can be resultant health problems for the individual who is trying to cope with this. Alternatively, the individual may stay away from work, and the absenteeism then becomes a problem for the organisation. The Confederation of British Industries (CBI) estimated in 1994 that stress currently costs British industries in the region of five billion pounds a year. The costs to the individual worker are equally devastating (see Box 6.1).

Box 6.1 The costs of a health-endangering workload

John Walker worked for Northumberland County Council as a social worker and suffered a breakdown due, he told his employers, to an unreasonably heavy workload. He returned to work, and initally his employers provided additional staff to ease the workload. However, shortly afterwards, these were taken away, leaving John with the same heavy workload which had caused his first illness. When he suffered a breakdown again, he subsequently sued his employers for putting him in a situation which was known to have endangered his health previously. In November 1994, the High Court ruled that Northumberland County Council had failed in its duty of care to provide a safe workplace by failure to take reasonable steps to avoid exposing John Walker to a health-endangering workload.

Law Report, Queen's Bench Division, 24 November 1994.

Models of stress

In trying to understand stress, psychologists and doctors produced models. One of the first of these was called the **Engineering model**, which viewed stress as a force which acted on the individual. When the stress became too great, the person 'snapped', in the same way that an overloaded bearing might break. This model viewed the individual as a passive receptacle for stress, which, of course, people are not. If we were, we would all be susceptible to the same stressors and break at the same point, as metals do. The model was inadequate in that it did not take into account the individual differences between people, and also the fact that they interact with – and sometimes wrestle with – their environments.

General Adaptation Syndrome

In 1956, Selye put forward a model called the General Adaptation Syndrome, describing the physiological changes which took place within the stressed individual. The heart rate and blood pressure increase, and adrenalin and noradrenalin are released in order to maintain the body's state of 'readiness' to fight an aggressor. The maintenance of these responses depletes the body's resources leaving it open to invasion by illness. If the stress continues long term, the individual suffers collapse and may die. Stress has been implicated in deterioration of the immune system, as well as cancer, heart attacks, other cardiovascular problems and digestive tract disturbances.

This sequence of phases, Selye suggested, was common to all individuals in response to any stressor. This assumption has been challenged on two counts; firstly, that responses vary between individuals, we do not all produce exactly the same physiological responses to stress, and secondly, that these may not be the same responses made by any individual in response to a number of different stressors. Cox et al. (1985) suggested that different amounts of noradrenalin and adrenalin are released in response to different stressors. Three different types of job task were studied, and the levels of noradrenalin and adrenalin excreted in the urine of the workers was subsequently measured. This was found to vary between subjects, depending on the job task at the time. Increases in noradrenalin related broadly to physical activities in the tasks and to constraints and frustration, while adrenalin increases were related to feelings of effort and stress.

Person-environment fit

The person-environment fit model of stress, proposed by French, Caplan and Van Harrison (1982), examined the interaction between the individual and the workplace environment. Identified as important were the extent to which the employee's abilities fitted the demands of the job, and how well the job environment fitted the employee's needs, especially the use of skills and abilities. This interactional model of stress did not allow for a number of other variables in the workplace, which may influence an individual's perception of how well he or she fits into that environment.

Transactional models

Currently, transactional models of stress appear to offer the best explanations of stress processes. There are a number of these (see Figure 6.1 opposite for an example). All include the concept that people are active in their own environment, that interactions take place which involve a number of variables, some of which prompt feelings of stress (e.g. work problems) or mitigate stress (e.g. social support from colleagues). This involves focusing on cognitive processes and emotional reactions of individuals to stress in their environments.

Cognitive processes involve the continuous monitoring of the stress situation, and the decisions made on coping methods. Lazarus and Folkman (1984) suggested that stress arises when individuals perceive that they cannot cope with demands being made upon them. This perceived inability to cope induces emotional responses, such as worry or depression. A number of researchers suggest that current stressors, such as stress at work, may have an additive effect with existing life stressors, such as coping with the effects of divorce. This will consequently make any work stress more difficult to cope with. Karasek (1979) suggests that the effect may not be simply additive, but multiplicative, due to the complex interactions of more than one stressor.

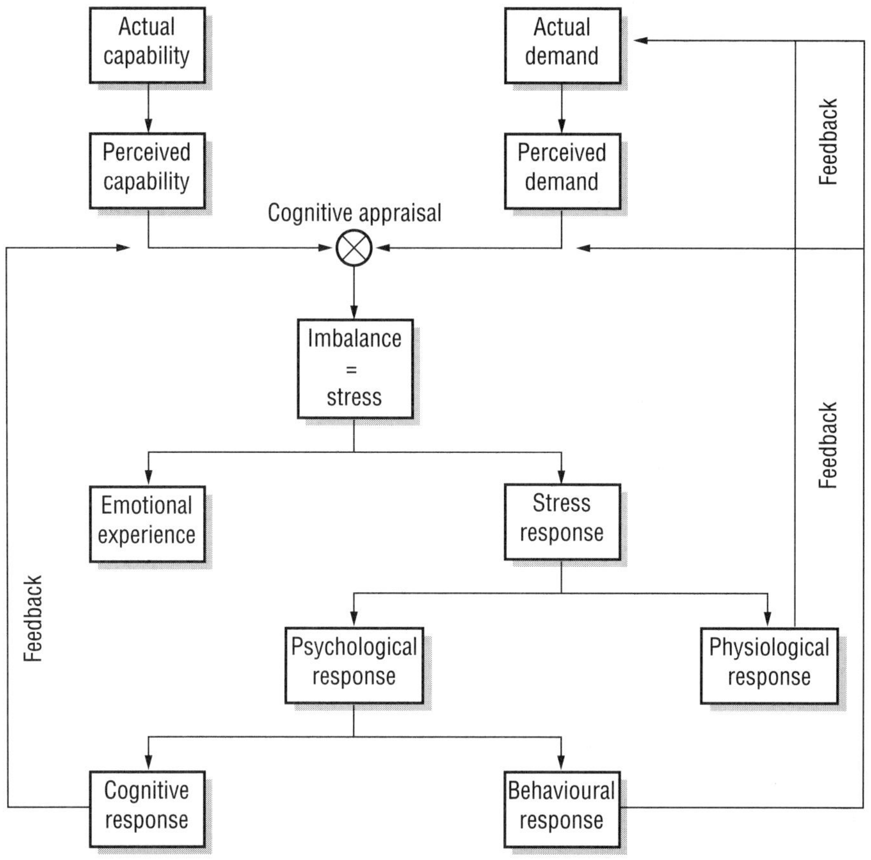

FIGURE 6.1 *Transactional Model of Stress (Cox and Mackay). From Stress (1978) by Tom Cox. Reproduced by permission of the publisher, Macmillan Press Ltd*

SOURCES OF STRESS

1 Long-term stressors

Changes occurring during a person's life may give rise to the experience of stress. If these are not resolved, chronic stress may result. Scales to measure these include the Social Readjustment Rating Scale (Holmes and Rahe, 1967) and the PERI Life Events Scale (Dohrenwend et al., 1988).

Box 6.2 The social readjustment rating scale

	Life Event	**Stress Value**
1	Death of spouse	100
2	Divorce	73
3	Marital separation	65
4	Jail term	63
5	Death of close family member	63
6	Personal injury or illness	53
7	Marriage	50
8	Fired at work	47
9	Marital reconciliation	45
10	Retirement	45
11	Change in health of family member	44
12	Pregnancy	40
13	Sex difficulties	39
14	Gain of new family member	39
15	Business readjustment	39
16	Change in financial state	38
17	Death of close friend	37
18	Change to different line of work	36
19	Change in number of arguments with spouse	35
20	Mortgage over $10,000	31
21	Foreclosure of mortgage or loan	30
22	Change in responsibilities at work	29
23	Son or daughter leaving home	29
24	Trouble with in-laws	29
25	Outstanding personal achievement	28
26	Wife begins or stops work	26
27	Begin or end school	26
28	Change in living conditions	25
29	Revision of personal habits	24
30	Trouble with boss	23
31	Change in work hours or conditions	20
32	Change in residence	20
33	Change in schools	20
34	Change in recreation	19
35	Change in church activities	19
36	Change in social activities	18
37	Mortgage or loan less than $10,000	17
38	Change in sleeping habits	16
39	Change in number of family get-togthers	15
40	Change in eating habits	15
41	Vacation	13
42	Christmas	12
43	Minor violations of the law	11

Source: T. H. Holmes and R. H. Rahe, 'The Social Readjustments Rating Scale,' *Journal of Psychosomatic Research*, 11 (1967), pp. 213–218.

Holmes and Rahe constructed their scale (see Box 6.2) by researching medical records of patients who suffered from illnesses after experiencing psychological trauma. These trauma, or life events, were ranked in order of severity, with 'Death of a spouse' being ranked 1, as most severe. These events were then assigned values which were weighted LCUs (Life Change Units). Individuals were asked to check off the number of life events which had happened to them in a specified time (say a year), and their total LCUs were calculated. Holmes and Rahe predicted that serious physical, stress-related illnesses were likely to follow high scores of 300 or above. Research to substantiate the link between life events and physical illnesses has not been conclusive, however. Tennant (1983) reviewed ten studies, only two of which demonstrated that LCU scores could predict subsequent illnesses. It is possible that the subsequent illnesses may be more specifically linked to the life events than early researchers recognised. A recent review (Finlay-Jones, 1988) concluded that life events involving loss were more likely to be followed by depressive illnesses, suicidal behaviour and mania, while life events involving danger were likely to be followed by anxiety states.

The PERI questionnaire contains work-related events. However, these have been construed by some researchers as being acute and discrete (e.g. being promoted/demoted) rather than chronic. This highlights the confusion which exists over the terms 'acute' and 'long-term' or 'chronic'. Arguably, the death of a spouse is a discrete event, causing acute stress, but the residual effects may be chronic. These may include the lowering of standards of hygiene, nutrition, housing and general self-maintenance in some individuals; others may adjust to a 'single' life with little or no detriment to standards of living. Individual responses to major life events (MLE) are one of the criticisms of using a scale for evaluating MLEs. However, where a large number of subjects are involved, self-ratings of life events show concurrence between raters (Dohrenwend *et al.*, 1988). For this reason, measures of life event stressors need to be taken into account when considering an overall picture of stress.

Cox (1993) suggests that most work-related stressors are chronic, but do not feature in life events scales. A method of identification and measurement for these needs to be constructed. Stress due to life events may interact with stresses occuring in the workplace, thereby intensifying their effect.

2 Daily hassles

Lazarus (1976) suggested that day-to-day hassles and uplifts (good events) would have a greater impact upon an individual's stress level (problems such as 'an inconsiderate smoker' or the 'rising price of goods'). Questions on potentially irritating aspects of day-to-day life are itemised on questionnaires such as the Hassles Scale. In a major study comparing participants' scores on a life events scale and their scores on the Hassles Scale with their subsequent physical health, DeLongis et al. (1982) found that hassles were more reliable than life events in predicting health outcomes. However, few items on the Hassles Scale are work-related items, which would seem to omit a large area for investigation.

3 Work stress

Cox et al. (1981) found that work was cited as the major source of stress and problems for fifty-four per cent of respondents, while a further twelve per cent cited the home/work interface. Therefore, occupational stress would seem to be an area necessitating investigation, commencing with areas of work which may be identified as potentially stressful.

Work overload/underload

A common source of stress at work is having too much to do or a job requiring excessive speed or output. This is quantitative overload, but overload can also be qualitative – having work which is too difficult or requires excessive concentration. High levels of anxiety and frustration were found among clerical workers who reported heavy workloads (Spector, 1987). Work underload is also stressful and results in boredom and frustration, suggested French and Caplan, (1972). This can also be quantitative (not enough to do) or qualitative (under-utilisation of the employee's skills and abilities). This work insufficiency has been found to be associated with psychological strain, low job satisfaction and low organisational commitment.

Role ambiguity and role conflict

Role ambiguity occurs when an employee is not clear as to his or her work role within the organisation. This is often demonstrated as confusion over objectives and expectations, and uncertainty about the scope and responsibilities associated with the job. Spector et al. (1988) found role ambiguity was associated with frustration and anxiety.

Role conflict may occur when an individual is asked to carry out a role which conflicts with their beliefs and values, or when they play various roles which are incompatible with each other. For example, a manager may be expected to increase production output of the section and also to provide work counselling to the employees; these two roles may not be incompatible, but may be perceived as such by some individuals. Shirom et al. (1989) found that there was a significant relationship between role conflict and the incidence of coronary heart disease among white-collar workers, but not among blue-collar workers. Those who work at the boundaries of organisations, between shop-floor and management, are likely to experience role conflict. Margolis and Kroes (1974) found that foremen were seven times more likely to develop digestive tract ulcers than were shop-floor workers.

Job insecurity and lack of career development

Job insecurity and redundancy are very real fears for many people. The sense of anxiety experienced is also heightened by the feeling of unfairness that the organisation still requires total commitment on the part of the employee, whilst this is not reciprocated by the organisation (Porter, 1990). Lack of career structures within organisations or fears that the individual has reached his or her promotional ceiling have been related to feelings of stress and poor physical health (Kasl and Cobb, 1982).

Decision latitude and control

Warr (1992) suggested that workers should ideally be able to plan their own workloads, to make decisions about work practices and take decisions as to how to tackle work problems. This kind of empowerment, it has been argued, can also be a source of stress, depending on the outcomes of the decisions to be made. However, the majority of research in this area suggests that low decision latitude and little control is associated with low self-esteem and low job satisfaction, anxiety, depression, feelings of stress, apathy and exhaustion, as well as physical symptoms of cardiovascular disease (Sauter et al., 1992; Ganster and Fusilier, 1989; Karasek and Theorell, 1990).

Interpersonal relationships

Good relationships at work promote health for the individual and the organisation. These may include relationships with superiors, subordinates and peers or colleagues. Relationships at work and outside the workplace are usually viewed as playing a moderating role, a buffer, on stressful situations. Karasek et al. (1982) studied over 1,000 male workers in Sweden and it was shown that support from supervisors and colleages buffered the effects of job demands and helped maintain job satisfaction. Low interpersonal support at work has been shown to be associated with high anxiety, job tension and low job satisfaction (Warr, 1992). Matteson and Ivancevich (1982) found the most common source of work stress was an inability to get on with other workers.

Bullying and violence at work is an issue which has recently been highlighted. Bullying may stop short of actual physical violence, but may cause such severe stress that individuals may absent themselves from work, suffer mental ill-health or leave the job. Cox and Leather (1994) argue for control of violence in the workplace through use of cognitive behavioural approaches, where the situation is appraised rather than apportioning blame to the individuals involved.

Home/work interface

A number of issues have been examined in this context. First, the obvious conflict of time demands between home and work, where research has centred mainly on working women. In these so-called days of equality, surveys show that women still carry out more household tasks and child care than their partners. Conflicting demands can be a source of stress if these are not resolved adequately (Bhagat and Chassie, 1981). In addition, social and emotional support from the partner may be affected by the conflicting demands of home and work (Cooper and Hingley, 1985).

In the broader area of 'non-work time', leisure pursuits may be affected for those workers who feel they have insufficient energy or time to participate in outside activities. Cox (1980) suggests that more is involved than just physically demanding jobs, the influence of repetitive work may be to deaden initiative.

4 Occupations

Some occupations are seen as more stressful than others. High on the list come medical professionals (doctors, pharmacists and nurses). A survey carried out by Wolfgang (1988) found nurses to have the highest levels of stress, measured by self-report questionnaires. In the United Kingdom, one of the highest occupational suicide groups is doctors, closely followed by farmers. If these suicides are related to stress, depression and anxiety, the reasons for both may be very different, but need investigation.

Managers and executives are often thought of as being susceptible to stress; indeed, the term 'executive stress' has fallen into everyday usage. However, research would seem to suggest that organisational design, level of management and country of origin all define which managers are stressed. Cooper and Hensman (1985) surveyed the mental health and stress levels of senior executives from ten countries and found that those from developing countries (Brazil and Egypt, for example) showed more stress than those from developed countries, such as Sweden or Germany. The researchers suggested that lack of autonomy in their work responsibilities appeared to be the source of their stress. In an extension of the international comparison, McCormick and Cooper (1988) compared New Zealand executives with those from other countries and found low stress levels. This was attributed to the relaxed lifestyle in that country.

A number of other surveys of different strata of management have suggested that middle management are particularly prone to stress. Ivancevich et al. (1982) suggested this was attributable to work overload and role conflict.

Air-traffic controllers are an occupational group recognised as having a high-stress job, and this has been confirmed by a number of researchers. A cross-cultural study by Shouksmith and Burrough (1988) compared self-reported stress levels of Canadian air-traffic controllers with their New Zealand counterparts and found their stress levels were equally high. Both groups cited fear of causing accidents, equipment limitations, heavy workload during peak traffic and poor work environment as stressors.

Police officers would appear to have a stressful job, but surveys taken are not always in agreement with this concept. In a study comparing their responses with those of health-care professionals, Maslach and Jackson (1981) found less evidence of emotional exhaustion (burnout) in police officers. Later studies (Gaines and Jermier, 1983; Jermier et al., 1989) found that officers expressed more stress due to inflexible procedures rather than danger on the job, which seemed to be a element associated with task variety.

Burnout

Burnout is an extreme form of stress, associated with the human service and caring professions, such as nursing or social work. Individuals suffering from burnout are physically fatigued, feel depersonalised and emotionally exhausted and believe that they can no longer care adequately for those whom they are looking after. Maslach and Jackson (1981) even identified callous behaviour in those suffering from burnout. Work stressors such as role conflict and work overload contribute to the development of burnout and lack of social support at work has been found to be associated with the experience (Jackson et al., 1987).

5 Environmental stressors

Environmental stressors may be acute or chronic. They include such problems as noise, which was discussed in the previous chapter as a health-related problem, in both the physical and psychological dimensions. Smith (1995) reviewed research into the non-auditory effects of noise and suggested that stress was a result of constant exposure to noise in the workplace.

Poor physical working conditions in general were found to affect workers' physiological and psychological health, which resulted in the experience of stress, according to a study carried out by Warr (1992).

Extremes of temperature and humidity were also found to be related to increased stress levels (Biersner et al. 1971). A more recent study by Meese et al. (1984) demonstrated gender differences in response to temperatures at work. Factory workers were asked to work full shifts in a range of controlled temperatures, performing manual tasks. All work was adversely affected at low temperatures, down to 6 degrees centigrade. Males worked best at 32 degrees centigrade, but females worked best between 20 to 26 degrees. The temperature measured in this study was ambient (room) temperature. Possibly if core body temperatures were taken, smaller differences would be observed.

6 Work times

Constantly working to schedules and deadlines can be a source of stress. Working long hours, in excess of sixty hours per week, is related to physical illness and psychological breakdown (Cooper, 1995). Shift work disrupts the circadian rhythym, which puts stress on the body, while family life may be disrupted by shift changes; both are liable to result in stress. Unpredictable work hours are also seen as stressful, possibly because the element of control over going to work and returning home has been removed.

MODERATING VARIABLES

Differences between individuals and their circumstances affect the level of stress experienced in response to a stressor. Important varibles identified include social support and personality characteristics. These modify the impact of a stressor, which is why they are termed 'moderator variables'; they are discussed below. In order to fully understand the effects of stress on the individual, moderator variables need to be measured and considered in an overall understanding of stress in the workplace.

Psychosocial support

From research evidence, it would appear that social support is necessary in each major area of an individual's life. For most people, this would include two main areas: work and home. The support of family and friends has been recognised for some time as a buffer for stress. Investigations and surveys in the workplace (Karasek, et al. 1982) have shown that support from supervisors and colleagues affects the perceptions of job demands and job satisfaction, while Ganster et al. (1986) demonstrated that social support offsets the effects of adverse working conditions. Low social support at work has been shown to be associated with negative events, such as job tension, high anxiety and increased risk of cardiovascular disease (Warr, 1990).

A recent study in the Netherlands (van der Pompe and de Heus, 1993) investigated work-related areas of stress for eighty male and seventy-five female managers. Only work support was strongly related to reducing work stress on each of the measures taken; social support from outside work areas was negatively related to depression. The study did not find that women experienced more stress and strains than men, which contradicts the findings from some previous studies (for example, McDonald and Korabik, 1991).

Personal characteristics

Personal characteristics have been suggested by many as the underlying reason why individuals react so differently to stressors. What is seen as a disaster by some people is taken in their stride by others. As a variable, vulnerability needs to be investigated, by enquiring into personality characteristics which have been previously identified as associated with stress. Henderson (1981) found that personality variables were the most important source of variance in stress-related illness. There is no shortage of personality tests, claiming to identify a number of traits, types and dispositional variables. Furnham (1992) points out that some models of stress suggest personality variables are the precursor to stress, while others see personality as moderating the impacts of stressors; all regard individual differences as important in the experience of stress.

Neuroticism

Neuroticism describes how stable or unstable a person's mental state is. A number of tests claim to measure this concept, including Eysenck's Personality Inventory.

The relationship of neuroticism to perceived stress and health symptoms has been reported by a number of investigators. Watson and Pennebaker (1989) found a positive correlation between an individual's self-reported (perceived) stress level and neuroticism as measured by psychometric tests. A high level of self-reported symptoms of ill health correlated with neuroticism.

Type A personality

Type A personalities were identified by Friedman and Rosenman (1974) as being susceptible to the effects of stress. Type A personalities are always in a hurry, cannot wait for anything and are highly competitive, not only at work but during their leisure activities. From a study undertaken in 1974, they suggested that individuals who display Type A behaviours are two and a half times more likely to suffer heart attacks or develop cardiovascular disease than those who do not display these behaviours. Because Type As are so competitive and 'driven', they are likely to be highly successful in their work, which means that their organisation will encourage their activities, possibly without realising they may be endangering their health, if not their lives. Type B personalities, Friedman and Rosenman suggest, may be equally ambitious, but do not behave in such a 'driven' manner; they are not so competitive and are more relaxed about time.

Hardiness

Hardiness is an attribute which enhances an individual's ability to reduce the impact of stressful events. The 'hardy personality' was identified by Kobasa as someone who experiences problems and adverse life events which, in other individuals, might be expected to lead to stress. Hardiness (Kobasa, Maddi and Kahn, 1982) is thought to be a tripartite structure, comprising Control, Commitment and Challenge, all of which are useful to the individual in the workplace as processes in the control and reduction of stress.

Self-esteem

Self-esteem describes how highly an individual regards him- or herself, whether this is realistic or not. A number of correlational studies have shown low self-esteem to be related to depression (for example, Ormel, Sanderman and Stewart, 1989; Beck, 1967). As depression has been shown to be associated with stress, it follows that low self-esteem may also be implicated in stress.

Greenberg et al. (1992) suggested that low self-esteem is also correlated with high anxiety. In a series of experiments, self-esteem was manipulated, participants were exposed to threat and their anxiety levels subsequently measured. Those who had had their self-esteem increased showed less self-reported anxiety to threat than those whose self-esteem was not raised.

Locus of control

This concept was introduced by Rotter (1966). An individual with an external locus of control believes that life is largely controlled by external factors or events, whereas people with an internal locus of control believe that the control over their lives is centralised in themselves. Direct evidence linking locus of control with stress is unclear, but a number of researchers (e.g. Greenberg, op. cit.; Thompson, 1981) have suggested that an internal locus of control may be associated with high self-esteem levels and the overall concept of controllability of potential stressors, in order to reduce stress.

Measuring stress

It is difficult to evaluate research into stress, because of the problems involved with measuring stress in the first place. In addition, there are so many facets involved in the stress process, it would be possible to miss an influential variable. Another criticism levelled at research into stress is that it is mainly cross-sectional in design and therefore gives an incomplete picture of what happens to the individual who is suffering from stress. Many of the health-related effects of stress (heart disease, cancer) are not apparent until some time after the stressful event has passed.

Stress levels (self-report measures)

There are a number of self-report questionnaires available to indicate an individual's stress levels. For example, Cooper's Occupational Stress Inventory enquires into a number of areas, such as feelings about the individual's job, sources of job pressure, current state of mental and physical health, job and health-related behaviours.

As stress can be involved with either depression or anger and frustration, it could be seen as useful to select measures which would encompass both of these, in order to give a complete picture.

Test publishers supply data on the reliability and validity of tests, together with scoring norms for most occupational groups.

Validity

This asks whether the test really examines what it is supposed to test; that is, whether a test measuring stress is really telling you something about an individual's level of stress.

Reliability

Whether the test will reliably produce the same result with the same individual, if retested, provided no changes have occurred in that individual's life.

Perceived stress levels

Perceived stress levels are the result of self-appraisal, enquiring into one's own feelings and experiences of stress. Previous research has shown that, while a number of people may be subject to the same stressor, not all of them perceive it to be stressful. Cohen (1983, 1986) suggests that it is these perceptions of stress which are potentially harmful, rather than the total number of stressors to which an individual is subject. Cohen's PSS (Perceived Stress State) enquires into the perceived levels of stress by separating subjective from objective components. This measure could be usefully compared with other self-report mood state measures.

Physiological Indices

Heart rate and blood pressure are elevated, and galvanic skin responses change, in response to stress. However, these have been shown to be unreliable measures to take as 'objective' measures of stress. Generally, there are no measures available for individuals from the time before they entered the stressed state; therefore, no comparisons can be made with their normal state. In addition, these physiological mechanisms are liable to change for other reasons – the person may have just run up the stairs! Measures of hormones such as adrenalin and noradrenalin are not wholly reliable for the same reasons. In addition, taking blood samples from people, in order to assess stress, is enough to raise stress levels in many people. Cortisol levels appear to provide a reasonably stable measure in relationship to stress and can be assessed from saliva, but this still does not overcome the criticism that pre-stress levels are unlikely to be available in the real-life situation.

Overview of measuring stress

While both self-report questionnaires and (so-called) objective physiological measures are available for measuring stress, there are criticisms levelled at all of these. With regard to self-report questionnaires, you are simply obtaining that subject's perception of his or her own stress, which may be biased. There are researchers who would argue that it is the subject's own analysis of the stress levels which is important, as stress is a subjective experience. However, it has not been clearly demonstrated by medical research whether the physiological correlates of stress continue to increase even when the subjective perceptions do not. If this is so, the health of individuals is likely to suffer because they have not perceived themselves to be stressed. Organisations can only be aware of this possibility and do all in their power to ensure that stressful environments at work are carefully controlled.

THE EFFECTS OF WORK STRESS

The effects of work stress are both physical and psychological. Some common stress-related illnesses may be: colitis, high blood pressure, heart disease, ulcers, respiratory illnesses, migraine headaches and some forms of cancer. Some of these can be life-threatening, so the seriousness of stress should not be underestimated.

Stress also affects people's psychological states. It is associated with depression, anxiety and chronic fatigue (but not chronic fatigue syndrome, which is understood to be virus-induced). Stress will affect work performance. It may reduce output, cause accidents, reduce job satisfaction and demotivate workers. The long-term effects of this may be to cause absenteeism through physical or psychological ill-health, or increase job turnover, as employees leave work in order to reduce their stress. These outcomes are costly, not only to the individual, but also to the organisation.

MANAGING AND COPING WITH STRESS

Coping with stress is what everyone does, or tries to do, with varying levels of success, when reacting to a stressor. Managing stress is pro-active; the individual recognises stress and takes positive steps to deal with it.

Coping responses may be adaptive or maladaptive (in other words, either of long-term benefit to the individual or detrimental to the individual in the long run). Examples of maladaptive coping responses include the use of alcohol or other drugs, which may seem to help the individual to cope in the short term, but may lead to a decline in physical and mental health. If taken in the workplace, they can predispose the individual to make mistakes which could lead to accidents or other serious consequences, both for workers and the organisation. Other maladaptive coping responses, such as denial that a problem exists, are only temporary, and sooner or later, the problem has to be faced – prevarication (putting off) usually only makes matters worse.

Adaptive processes include seeking social support, either from colleagues in work-based problems, or within the family or social circle. Social support is therefore seen as a moderating process, buffering stressors as they arise, and as a process for helping the individual deal with specific situations after they have arisen.

Organisational coping or managing strategies can be undertaken by organisations to reduce stress at source for employees. Altering job design or workplace design so that it is more user-friendly, or improving person-job fit by matching employees' skills to the tasks they perform, are a few simple ways in which the organisation can cost-effectively reduce stress. Improving communications within the organisation and increasing employees' decision latitude and sense of control, together with the elimination of punitive management techniques, will increase job satisfaction and thereby reduce stress and increase the quality of work life.

Stress management programmes may be offered, either privately, or by organisations for their employees. These may concentrate on one single method or present a number of methods shown to reduce stress. The objectives may be either the prevention of the experience of stress, through promoting adaptive behaviours, or rehabilitation, to assist those who are experiencing stress to find the best (adaptive) methods of coping. A number of methods are offered. Psychosomatic methods include relaxation, meditation or biofeedback. Time management helps individuals prioritise demands made upon them, although of course, it cannot solve the problem of work overload. Assertiveness training is sometimes offered. This greatly assists those whose stress is a result of being 'put upon', or who are subject to sexual harassment, which may also be a cause of stress. Cognitive appraisal helps an individual to recognise his or her stressors and helps to deconstruct thought processes which may be making stress worse. Physical exercise has been recognised as one of the most effective methods of stress management, and some programmes include this. In fact, it could easily become a feature of organisational life – it is cheap, clean and cost effective – yet it seems to be promoted very little in the workplace.

Employee Assistance Programmes (EAPs) have been set up by a number of organisations, to help employees under stress. These consist primarily of counselling with trained counsellors who will provide a listening service and, if necessary, advice on workplace and home problems. (A description of workplace counselling appears in Chapter 7.) By offering a range of methods of stress management, the programme would appear to have more likelihood of success, for the same method is unlikely to suit everyone (Auerbach, 1989). Research suggests that programmes spread over a number of weeks have more impact than programmes presented entirely in one day, even when total presentation hours are equal. This would seem to be reasonable, given that the aim is to change a person's behaviour in response to stressors; behaviour changes are more easily affected over time, not in one day.

Many reviews have stated that most stress management programmes are aimed at managerial and white-collar staff. These emphasise the need for the individual to change in order to fit the work situation, which may be a reflection of management views in many countries (Murphy, 1988; Ivancevich et al., 1990). Union groups see organisational problems and work practices as causing stress, therefore job design and managerial style need intervention. It may be that, as so often in psychology, the truth is a 'bit of both'. It would be maladaptive for the wrangling to impede the welfare of the individual.

The effectiveness of interventions is difficult to evaluate. It would necessitate taking pre-intervention and post-intervention measures of stress and seeing whether stress was lower on the post-intervention measures. However, people live in the real world and may have been subject to undetected stressful events when one or other of the measures were taken, thereby invalidating results. Additionally, it is very difficult to identify which measures most accurately reflect an individual's stress. The variability of stress management programmes themselves makes their evaluation specific only to each particular study.

Post-Traumatic Stress Disorder (PTSD)

This is a delayed or protracted response to a major stressful event or disaster. It may have involved the individual as a participant or a witness to, for example, a serious accident, earthquake, war or violent death of others. Symptoms include repeatedly reliving the trauma (flashbacks), emotional blunting, detachment from others, fear and avoidance of cues associated with the original trauma. Anxiety and depression are often associated with PTSD.

In an occupational setting, PTSD could result from witnessing or being involved in major work accidents. Some occupations, such as medical professionals, police, firefighters and armed services may have to face major traumas as part of their job. This does not absolve them from the effects of PTSD – in fact, it may serve to make it worse. After an earthquake in Armenia, two groups of rescue workers, one consisting of trained firefighters, the other of volunteers with little or no experience, were examined for PTSD (Paton, 1990). The volunteers displayed a lower level of all symptoms than the professionals. Paton suggested this may have been due to higher expectations in the professionals that they would be able to save lives, and disappointment at being unable to do so.

SUMMARY

Not all sources of stress affect individuals equally, or in the same way; there is an interaction between the individual and the stress source. Factors such as personality differences, or the amount of social support an individual receives, can exacerbate or relieve stress problems. The measurement of stress is difficult, both physiologically and psychologically, and often goes unrecognised until the individual breaks down or becomes seriously ill.

Stress in the workplace may be due to a number of different causes, but needs to be recognised and dealt with, both at the organisational level, by improved management techniques, and at the individual level, by helping employees to recognise and manage stress effectively.

chapter seven
ORGANISATIONAL CHANGE AND DEVELOPMENT

CHAPTER OVERVIEW

This chapter outlines why organisations need to change and describes the dynamic influences within an organisation and external to that organisation. It seeks to demonstrate how one organisation's culture may differ from another's. Models of organisational change, arising from research, are outlined, in order to show some ways in which planned change might be effected.

INTRODUCTION: WHY ORGANISATIONS NEED TO CHANGE

Organisations consist of people; people constantly change in order to develop their lives and adapt to changing environments, not only at work, but at home, in leisure pursuits, in enlarging their family and network of friends and acquaintances. People who do not change tend to stagnate, withdraw inside themselves and lose contact with others.

Organisations are like individuals in these respects; development is an ongoing process. An organisation which is static is likely to become a failure. It needs to constantly update its production processes, keep abreast of new technology, review its procedures and educate its workforce. A dynamic organisation is one which is constantly changing in order to meet new challenges – in fact, to be ready before these challenges arise. Organisational development is a process of managing change, to achieve the goals (prescribed and implied) of that organisation. This should be achieved without the employees feeling threatened or undervalued. In fact, their own personal career needs should be integrated into the organisational changes being implemented. This is where Human Resource Planning becomes involved, training and deploying existing staff to utilise their skills, in order to assist organisational effectiveness. Psychological knowledge and skills are invaluable in effecting these changes, because informed insights into human behaviour allow for suitable techniques and programmes of change to be introduced.

ORGANISATIONAL DYNAMICS

External forces

Every organisation is constantly interacting with external forces, such as competitors and suppliers of raw goods, as well as local, national and international economic forces. These factors are summarised in Figure 7.1.

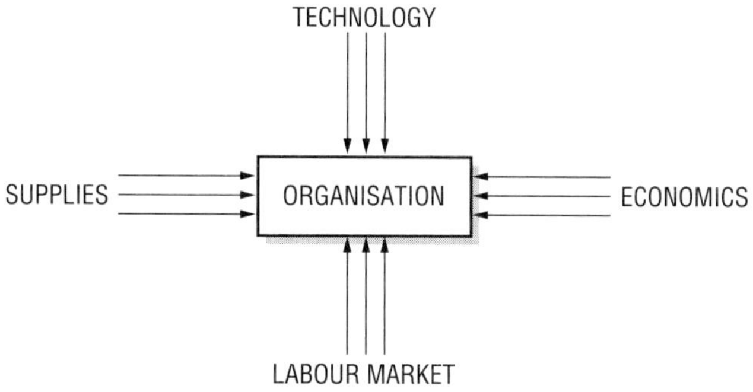

FIGURE 7.1 *External forces acting on the organisation*

Internal forces

Within each organisation, there are a number of systems which interact dynamically. Obviously important is the input/output process which is the core operation for that organisation. For a manufacturing industry, that process could be summarised as in Figure 7.2 as a main processing system with sub-systems; for example, a transport system and an accountancy/secretarial system. Information and marketing systems would also link into the main and sub-systems.

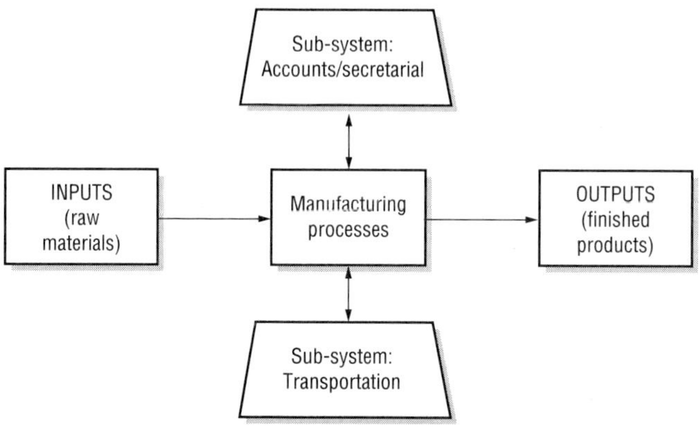

FIGURE 7.2 *Dynamics of a manufacturing organisation*

DYNAMIC PROCESSES WITHIN THE ORGANISATION

In addition to the formal process systems to be found within organisations, there are informal systems, such as social groups, and formal structures, such as work systems. Kotter (see Figure 7.3) suggests that these are all peripheral to a central core, which he calls **Key Organisational Processes**. These include:

- **Information-gathering**. Information is gathered externally from a number of sources: existing and potential customers, competitors, raw goods suppliers, markets. In addition, information is gathered internally from

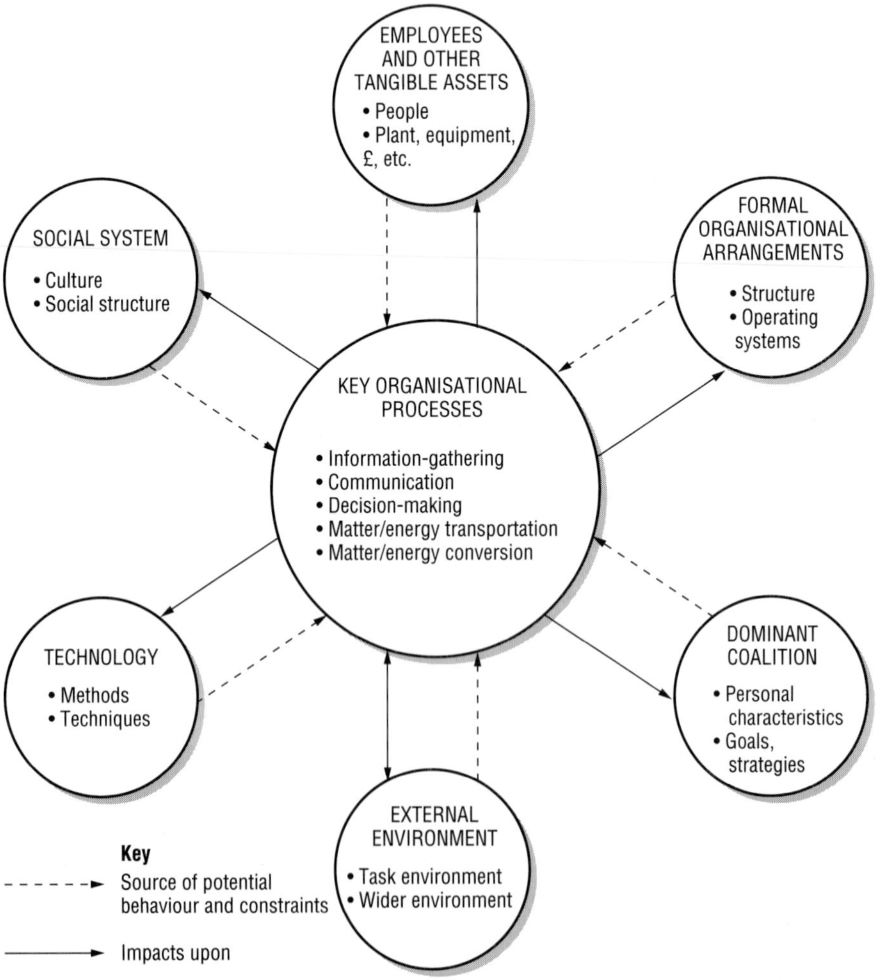

FIGURE 7.3 *Kotter's Model of Organisational Dynamics*

employees and managers on a number of matters, for example, work processes, new and existing machinery and technology.

- **Communication**. Information is disseminated around the organisation by formal systems, which may include written memoranda, letters and staff newsletters, and also verbally, through formal staff meetings, lectures and in-service days. Informally, most organisations also have a 'grapevine', by which information is communicated and sometimes distorted. It is better for organisations to communicate information promptly, especially about proposed changes, rather than allow distortion to take place, which will later have to be corrected.
- **Decision-making**. As a rule, decision-making processes are at management level, and decisions are fed downwards through the organisation's structure. Union decisions may also be taken which would affect a major part or the whole of an organisation. Where work groups are autonomous, decisions can be made at that level, for that particular group, provided the decision does not affect other groups; the issue would then become central, rather than group based.
- **Matter/energy transporting**. The organisation needs to set up a system of transport for inputs and outputs. These may be tangible items, for example sheet metal and coal, or energy outputs, such as electricity from a power station.
- **Matter/energy conversion**. These are the manufacturing processes instanced as central in the simplified diagram in Figure 7.2.

Kotter suggests that there are sub-systems around these central Key Organisational Processes.

Employees and other tangible assests

The human resources of the organisation are part of a system of assets, which also includes plant, machinery, office and other equipment, and monetary assets.

Formal organisational arrangements

This includes the structure of the organisation, in whatever form this takes (as discussed in Chapter 1). All operating systems utilised by the organisation are included here; for example, ordering systems for goods and services, marketing systems, customer-care systems and employee-care systems.

Dominant coalition

The personal characteristics of those in control of the organisation impinge upon the Key Organisational Processes, but are reciprocally influenced by those processes; it is a two-way interaction between management and organisation. The goals and strategies of the organisation similarly interact. All organisations need goals (as do individuals), otherwise lack of direction results in meandering and lack of achievement. Realistic goals have to be set for each organisation; unrealistic goals will not be met, with demoralising results.

Technology

The technological methods and techniques currently in use by the organisation impact upon the Key Organisational Processes. If those are out of date, then functions and possibly productivity may be limited. When technological systems are updated, methods have to be changed accordingly; this may well necessitate the training or re-training of personnel, which may in turn meet with some problems or resistance within the organisation.

Social system

There are a number of social systems within any organisation, both formal and informal. The culture of the organisation (discussed in the next section of this chapter) is usually an unwritten code, but is universally accepted within the organisation. The social structure of the organisation is often derived from its formal structure (described in Chapter 1). There are many sub-systems of the social structure, including work groups, friendship groups (which may arise simply because people arrived on the same day and were inducted together) and semi-formal social groups, such as the company's football team.

Dynamic interactions between organisation and environment

1 Lawrence and Lorsch's contingency model

Lawrence and Lorsch (1967) researched a number of industries in order to identify what made some organisations more successful than others. They found that if an organisation exists in an unstable environment (through uncertainty of supplies, customers or other environmental factors), then management style needs to be diverse and flexible, and the organisation must integrate departments which need to interact. Management style is contingent upon the environmental factors existing at any one time.

2 Galbraith's information processing model

Galbraith (1973) saw the organisation as an information-processing system. The information it processes comes from the environment, concerning inputs, outputs and labour availability. As such, Galbraith saw the organisation, rather than the environment, as uncertain, which was the view of the contingency model. Organisations can reduce uncertainty in a number of ways, Galbraith suggested. The environment might be stabilised by taking charge of input sources, by buying up a supplier, for instance. Internal changes can produce reductions in uncertainty – self-contained work units may stabilise production and quality. Decision-making can be decentralised, so that the bureaucratic processes of large organisations do not slow down necessary technological changes.

SUMMARY – ORGANISATIONAL DYNAMICS

In order to survive, an organisation is constantly changing. Forces which interact to bring about these changes may be external or internal. There are a number of systems which interact within an organisation and changes to any one of these may necessitate changes in other systems. Models of organisational dynamics, such as Kotter's, suggest ways in which these systems are divided and interact. Whether formal or informal, these all impact upon the functioning of the organisation. Changes in any one area may reflect through the key central areas and require changes in other systems. Dynamic forces in the environment act upon the organisation so structure and management need to recognise and adapt to these forces.

ORGANISATIONAL CULTURE

Schein (1990) suggests that organisational culture is becoming an increasingly important concept. It is irretrievably bound up with fundamental strategies of current functioning, such as recruitment, selection, training, socialisation and reward systems. Any programmes directed at change must take the organisation's culture into account or be doomed to failure.

What is organisational culture?

An organisation's culture can be briefly described as the pattern of norms and attitudes held within that organisation. These frequently reflect the pattern of leadership and structure of that organisation, which may not be the 'official norms' if the leaders do not adhere to them. For example, if the organisation's Mission Statement (a statement of aims and objectives) itemises aims of honest dealing, but the management are seen as being corrupt, the culture is more likely to echo that corruptness than the official line of honesty.

Determining an organisation's culture

Culture emanates from management levels, Schein (1987) suggests. He indicates three main levels of culture: artefacts, values and basic underlying assumptions.

Artefacts

These include such things as 'dress code'. Do people wear suits or casual clothes to work? Are suits for management level, and overalls or casuals for shop-floor workers? Where dress code is a strong artefact, it would probably be considered as 'wrong' for a shop-floor employee to wear a suit, as for the Managing Director to appear in a set of overalls, whereas in other companies, dress code is not considered important.

Another artefact giving cultural indications is the way in which people address each other within the organisation. Is everyone on first-name terms, indicating an egalitarian outlook? Are managers addressed as 'Mr Smith' or 'Mrs Jones', while other employees are addressed by first names, indicating carefully maintained strata? Or is everyone addressed formally?

Layout of the workplace also gives information regarding organisational culture. The introduction of 'open-plan' offices and work places a few years back was designed to imply egalitarianism. However, in large areas, the volume of noise made them almost unworkable. Modifications of the open-plan approach may now be used.

Values

The values of an organisation are the norms, ideologies and philosophies it supports. Some are available to all organisations: fair trading, honesty, integrity. Others may be specific to certain types of organisations: one car manufacturing company may pride itself on producing the cheapest car, another the best quality car, regardless of cost. Electricity does not aspire to changes in quality of product, but one company may aim for low price, another for high quality service. Customer care and employee care usually have norms which are specific to each organisation and which vary widely.

Basic underlying assumptions

These are often vague and not often consciously assessed. Employees may assert, 'This is a good/bad organisation to work for', but may have difficulty verbalising *why* they think this. Careful questioning may elicit tangible reasons, such as employees share options, or vague reasons such as, 'They don't seem to care about their employees'.

Frequently, basic underlying assumptions determine behaviours within an organisation. For example, petty pilfering from an employer is seen as acceptable and proliferates among employees in some organisations, but is rare in other similar organisations.

Maintaining an organisation's culture

Organisations tend to maintain their culture by a number of methods, including staff selection, training and socialisation of new employees.

Staff selection

Organisations may select new employees on the basis of similarity to existing employees (this is called **organisational cloning**). Organisational culture will be preserved more easily in this way, because these 'similar' employees will be predisposed to assimilating the culture which is in operation. Conversely, if the organisation requires a change of culture, new staff may be selected on the basis of new criteria which would seem to match the new corporate aims. For example, if you require a health service which is cost-effective and management-oriented, these are the qualities you select in new employees. The qualities of compassion and caring, possibly previous criteria, may be incompatible with these, and the culture will reflect this accordingly.

Training

New training methods may be instigated, both for new and existing staff, which emphasise the desired facets of the new organisational culture. For example, if an organisation is changing to new technology, re-training will be necessary for existing staff; this may be an ideal opportunity to re-shape the organisation's culture to one of fast-paced, high-tech, go-getting industry, if that is the desired cultural change.

Socialisation

Culture is learned. It is passed from employee to employee at all levels, either explicitly or implicitly, by behavioural, cognitive and emotional processes. These reflect the components of attitudes recognised by psychologists which, once learned, are resistant to change. Hirschorn (1987) suggests that the common assumptions held in organisations provide stability and reduce anxiety, in the way that defence mechanisms function within the individual. In this way, the socialisation of new employees would serve the individuals as well as the organisation.

Summary – Organisational culture

An organisation's culture is defined by artefacts, values and basic underlying assumptions, Schein suggests. These are created by management and learned by new employees. Once learned, these are difficult to change, although they will change and evolve over time as a natural evolutionary process. The change process may be advanced, in terms of culture, by selecting new staff who are seen as potentially favourable to the new culture, and by carefully selected training programmes.

ORGANISATIONAL CHANGE: THEORIES AND MODELS

So far, we have discussed changes within organisations, processes, systems and culture, as subject to natural changes over time. When radical change is perceived as necessary for an organisation, or when changes have to be accelerated, planned change becomes necessary in order to smooth the path of progress.

In recent years, in the UK, many organisations have had to adopt changes with major impact, due to changes in the economic situation and in government policies. For example, in the public sector, Colleges of Further Education are now totally independent of Local Education Authorities, and have to balance their own budgets, as do Hospital Trusts and universities, and utilities, such as water and electricity companies. In the private sector, many companies are merging or 'downsizing' (employing fewer staff), either through natural wastage or redundancies. Fewer staff means that jobs and systems often have to be totally reorganised.

If these changes are to be brought about efficiently and without too much opposition from existing employees and managers, then changes need to be managed carefully. Changes may be made at micro-level (changes in individuals' attitudes, training and jobs) or at macro-level (changes in an organisation's goals, structure or power balance). A number of theories and models of change exist; here we will examine just a few.

1 Lewin: a micro perspective

Lewin (1947) suggested that, in order to change work practices there should be a three-stage process: unfreezing, changing, freezing. Unfreezing involves stimulating people to recognise the need for change. The second step incorporates changing through training or applying a new technique or programme. The freezing stage includes reinforcement to ensure that new behaviours, attitudes and skills become permanent.

This is a simple model which can be used with individuals or groups to bring about minor changes. Where the major changes of today are often necessary, the micro perspective is inadequate, because large numbers of people may be involved, as well as changes to systems and structures.

2 Leavitt: a structural, technological and humanistic approach

Leavitt (1964) emphasises the inter-relationships within an organisation (see Figure 7.4).

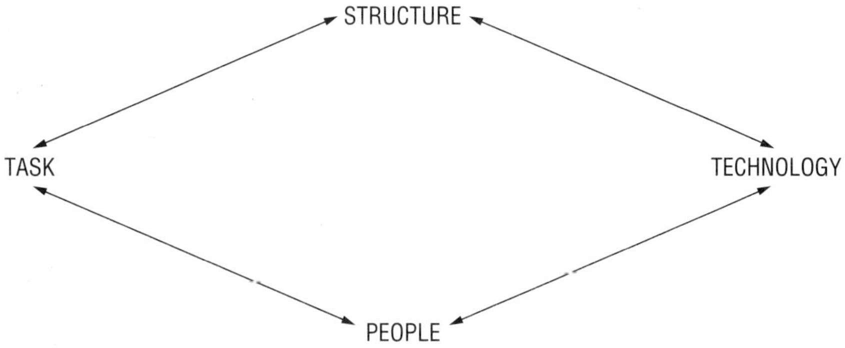

FIGURE 7.4 *Leavitt's approach to change. Changes in any one of these key areas will affect the other areas indicated*

The structure, people, technology and tasks of an organisation are so interdependent that if change is brought about in one area, it is bound to affect the other areas. Anyone planning changes should bear this in mind and be ready for repercussions and changes in other areas.

3 An economics approach to organisational development

Nord (1989) reviewed research into OD (Organisational Development) and suggested that the humanistic values which were the overt goals had not been achieved. Goals such as highly participative work environments, freedom of choice and control over decision-making, although aspired to, remained unfulfilled, often because of economic constraints. Lack of financial resources and economic strategies during the change operations, together with the reality that individuals usually operate on a self-interest basis, especially at work, meant that goals were often not achieved. The costs of change should be made explicit, with regard to existing economic and political situations. In future, Nord suggested, the factor of 'economics' should be added into the change equation.

4 A macro model of planned change

Szilagyi and Wallace (1990) suggest that the need for change may come from external forces, such as competitors, economic or political factors, or technological advances. Alternatively internal forces, such as a demoralised or inefficient workforce, may prompt change. Once problem areas are recognised and future goals identified, change is best managed by an agent, who will be trained specifically in the processes of change and will be less emotionally involved with the organisation than a manager.

The change agent identifies any constraints, such as resources and technology available, and also any resistance to change which may be encountered. An appropriate strategy for change is then selected and implemented, with careful attention to timing. Introducing a programme at the wrong time, or pushing ahead too quickly, can be disastrous in creating more problems than it solves. If change is carefully planned and implemented, new goals can be achieved.

5 Planned process model for OD and OT

If OD stands for Organisational Development, OT stands for Organisational Transformation. Porras and Silvers (1991) identified that some organisational changes were greater than development and involved transformation of the organisation. This needed to be recognised before change processes could be put in place (see Figure 7.5). The 'vision' provided for the transformation would include new beliefs and purposes. These would be translated into the work setting and the business of bringing about cognitive change would commence.

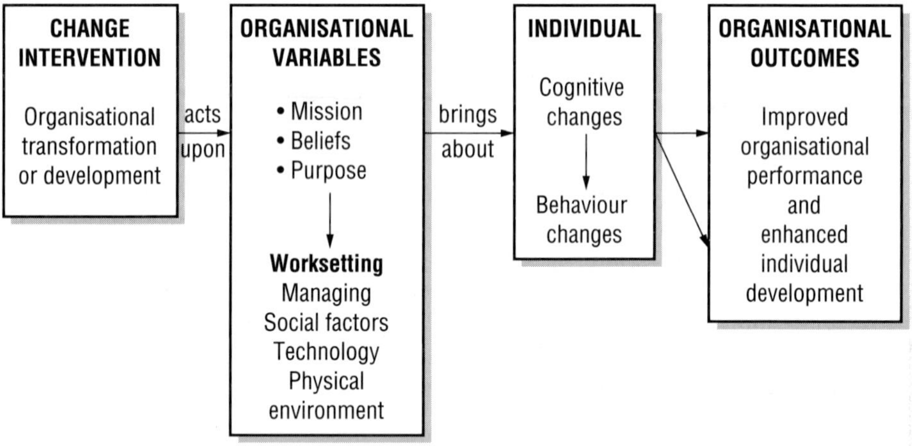

FIGURE 7.5 *A planned process model of change*

Assumptions are that individual behaviour is central to producing organisational outcomes (success/failure) and that individual work behaviour is prompted by the work-setting, which is designed by the organisation's 'vision'. Individual development and organisational performance are both derived from these behaviours.

A criticism of this model might be the lack of allowance made for external factors. However strong the 'vision', if political, social or economic forces from outside the organisation are unfavourable, OT and OD may be adversely affected.

Box 7.1 Managing organisational change at Jaguar cars

When Jaguar cars were made by British Leyland prior to 1991, morale was low and product quality was low. Jaguar was created as a separate company and morale rose, but quality was still low, due to pressure by BL for high productivity. This was the situation facing Ford Motors, who bought Jaguar because they wished to add a prestige product to their range. This is a brief outline of their change process.

1 **Identify problems and opportunities in the environment**
Opportunities: a market existed for prestige cars.
Problems: poor product quality; Jaguar was losing money as a company, which lowered workforce morale; workers were told there was a need for change or the company would have to close.

2 **Implications of problems**
The question of quality was addressed by researching all recent Jaguar owners to find out what problems they had experienced.

3 **Education for understanding**
From Board level to the shop-floor, all workers were made to realise that customers must be satisfied with the product. Briefing groups and meetings with union representatives were held to disclose and discuss boardroom plans.

4 **Getting involved**
All the workforce and managers at all levels became involved in the new plans to raise quality, change manufacturing methods and improve productivity.

5 **Setting targets**

- **Quality:** Jaguar was to have its own plant and suppliers – it was not to be regarded as a 'subsidiary'. Operatives were to be regarded as inspectors, in addition to the inspectors who were appointed. Monthly Quality Circles were set up to meet and identify problems arising. These were to be dealt with by the managers.
- **Production:** targets were set to rise for each worker, realistic with the new production methods.
- **Delivery:** target dates were to be met, to emphasise reliabilty of the company.

6 **Outcomes**
Corporate strategies were a success: Jaguar had autonomy, with the advantages of collaboration with a larger company in terms of technology; Ford had 'bought into' the luxury car market; employees now had the certainty of jobs continuing, morale was raised; shareholders were happy.

Goals of organisational change and development

More than just managing change, organisational development aims to align individuals' goals for career development with the organisation's goals. Planned change, over a given period of time, uses behavioural sciences to assist in the adjustment to change. Changes may be related to goals such as improved performance, increased motivation or co-operation, reduced absenteeism or staff turnover, reduced costs or minimised conflicts. Sensitive training methods, setting achievable goals and praise and reinforcement for appropriate behaviours will facilitate change.

How is planned change to be effected?

In recent years, there has been a terrific upsurge in bringing about changes in organisations, mainly driven by the technological advances made in commerce and industry. There are a number of ways of effecting change. The most appropriate method can be diagnosed by an organisational psychologist, bearing in mind the type of change necessary for the organisation and the workforce involved. Some of these methods include training, counselling and the use of power. These derive from different theoretical origins within psychology, and will be discussed in turn.

1 The use of power

Social psychology experiments in obedience, conformity and compliance demonstrated that people will obey the instructions of an individual seen as a powerful expert. In Milgram's (1963) experiments on obedience, participants were instructed to administer what they believed were electric shocks to another individual every time that person made a mistake. The level of shocks given far exceeded what would be expected, especially if the 'expert' were present, when even greater compliance was demonstrated by those giving the shocks.

Schein (1990) investigated the use of power within an organisation to bring about the changes seen as necessary. He found that the following steps may be used:

1 Leaders (i.e. management) highlight threats to the organisation if no change occurs. This may be information about economic pressure on the organisation which could necessitate loss of jobs, if changes are not made. Leaders encourage the idea that changes are not only possible, but desirable.
2 Leaders describe the new assumptions which will form the basis for the new direction the organisation is to take; they provide the new role models. This suggests that leaders are seen to change first.

3 Key positions are filled by new incumbents, who are not ingrained in the 'old ways'. They do not have to unlearn old practices, which is difficult, but can simply be trained in the new ways. This implies that existing employees who express doubts about or resistance to change, will not be promoted, but new people will be employed from outside. (There is a saying in OD, 'If you can't change the people, change the people'.)
4 Leaders systematically reward the new direction and 'punish' adherence to the old direction. This punishment may take the form of verbal correction or sending back work which does not comply with the new ways. Rewards may be praise, mention in House Journals, for example, or financial rewards such as bonuses.
5 The organisation's members are coerced or seduced into adopting new behaviours which are consistent with the new assumptions. Coercion can take the form of threats of demotion, pay loss or even job loss. Seduction is likely to be pay increases or improved benefits in other ways.
6 The 'sacred cows' of the organisation ('we have *always* done things this way') are discredited by the leaders, if those artefacts no longer fit the new scheme.
7 Leaders create new, emotionally-charged rituals and artefacts around the new assumptions, in order to replace the old ones.

This type of power-based change may work in organisations where the top management levels are seen as experts. As early as 1961, Burns and Stalker identified different management styles at a rayon mill, where expertise rested at the top of the organisation, and at an electronics company, where expertise in different areas permeated throughout the organisation. The former company may have been agreeable to 'top-down' ordered changes, but it is unlikely that the electronics company would. If blind obedience relies upon seeing the leader as 'expert', then only organisations which are 'top-down' driven will respond to this model of change.

Box 7.2 Misapplication of the power model

The power-based model was sorely misapplied in the UK recently, when Colleges of Further Education were told they were to become independent of local authorities. Almost overnight, principals who had been educationalists had to become managing directors, in essence. Few had any knowledge of business or economics, and even fewer had any knowledge of psychology. An advisory body was formed for them, in order to formulate and implement the changes seen as necessary. In order to made economic ends meet, it was deemed necessary that teaching staff should increase their class contact hours to an unspecified number and reduce their number of weeks' holiday, in order that more students (the raw materials which generated income) could be processed.

This unattractive package was obviously not well received, and Schein's model was followed, almost to the letter.

1 Principals highlighted the threat that other local colleges were now in direct competition with them, and they could close if they were not competitive.
2 New assumptions, that more students per class and fewer teaching hours per student would not result in falling standards, were suggested. There were few reports, however, of college principals providing role models by taking on additional teaching hours.
3 College departments or faculties underwent reorganisation, and management posts for these new areas were given to those who subscribed to the new regime or newcomers from outside.
4 Coercion took place, in that annual pay rises were suspended indefinitely until new contracts were signed, accepting the new conditions. On signing, a small pay rise was offered immediately, and annual increases would be reinstated. (Lack of annual pay rises in effect means a pay cut, as the cost of living continues to rise.)

This change strategy was not highly successful, as 'experts' are scattered throughout an entire college organisation. The organisational structure is a flat one, and employees perceive little difference between themselves and those at the top of the structure. But possibly the biggest mistake occured at the outset, in item 2. Teachers repudiated the assumption that bigger classes and more teaching hours would not damage standards. Because teachers are also emotionally involved with their jobs and 'believe' in education and the need for equality of opportunity for all, this change hit at the heart of their beliefs and values system, the component of attitudes which is hardest to change. Consequently, a great deal of animosity ensued, which needed a great deal of negotiation and give-and-take on both sides.

2 Training for change

Where individuals' jobs undergo change as a result of organisational changes, retraining may be necessary. This is often so when new machinery or technology is introduced. The introduction of computers revolutionised secretarial, accountancy and administative procedures, requiring new skills and making old skills redundant. This type of retraining needs careful management if people are not to feel devalued and to join the new schemes with enthusiasm. Giving people confidence to use their abilities in new situations is one of the aims of training.

In organisations such as the National Health Service, reorganisation has required people who were previously higher-grade nursing staff to become managers. Training programmes have been instigated to show them how to apply their skills of dealing with people, organising and administering procedures. In addition, they have the confidence that the decisions they make are the right ones.

A number of different training procedures are used in management training. One which most trainers agree brings out management skills and confidence to a high degree is outdoor training exercises. This is also extremely useful for team-building, a process used within organisations to introduce new teams who will work together or to cement existing teams.

Participants work in groups, in situations which are likely to be unfamiliar to all of them. No one is an 'expert', therefore everyone is on equal footing, although sometimes leaders emerge in various situations. Bales (1970) found that in unstructured groups who were given a task to achieve, two distinct leaders emerged: a task leader, who tended to be oriented towards achieving goals, and a socio-emotional leader, who supported the morale of the group. Outdoor exercise tasks must be geared to the potential capabilities of the group, in order that no one is injured. In addition, the task should be commensurate with the demands they are likely to meet as managers. Outcomes from these types of outdoor exercises (see Box 7.3 for an example) include increased confidence in the participants' own abilities, confidence in decision-making capabilities, a feeling of appreciation of the qualities of other team members, and the confidence that unknown situations can be tackled and conquered successfully.

Box 7.3 An example of an outdoor exercise task

Participants on a management training course were put into groups of six. They had met before, but not worked together as a team. All came from different organisations, so they had limited knowledge of each other's capabilities, interests or skills. In pairs, they were given brief training in either first aid, map reading or the use of caving equipment. They then had to disseminate this information to the others in their group within a given time. The task they were given was to rescue an 'injured' person (a confederate of the trainer) from a cave at a given map location, without worsening any injuries the caver said he had. They were allocated a minibus for transport and a driver who was not allowed to help them find the location of the cave. Once they had found the cave, expert cavers magically appeared out of the bushes, to observe the rescue. Needless to say, the 'cave' was not very deep, was high enough to stand up in and had a block end, to ensure no one got lost. In this type of exercise, participants will sometimes express fear of confined spaces, in which case groups will allocate them 'anchor' jobs at the mouth of the cave. They are frequently observed to enter the cave as though they are testing themselves. The aim of the task is to increase confidence, not overcome phobias, and 'heroics' are not expected.

3 Counselling for organisational change

Counselling has been used in the workplace for some time, to help employees with problems at work, at home or on the work/home interface. Increasingly of late, counselling has been used to smooth the path of organisational change. Its benefits are two-fold: it assists the employee to clarify perspectives on a new role within the organisation, and it assists the organisation, in that employees receiving counselling are less likely to be antagonistic to change, which can then proceed more effectively.

There are many forms of counselling, but it is outside the scope of this book to examine them all. Generally, the Rogerian tenets of genuineness, empathy and openness are held. The non-directive element of counselling is implicit in that it is better for individuals to see their own solutions to a problem rather than have suggestions made to them. However, when the agenda is organisational change, there is a need to steer in a particular direction. There is always a need to move on in counsellling, otherwise the counselling situation stagnates and becomes non-productive. Often goal-setting is used, the goals being expressed and set by the counsellor and client jointly.

In organisational settings, Egan's Helping Model (1994) (see Box 7.4) is often used. This model allows for a number of sessions between counsellor and client. It proceeds in stages, where goals are set and, when achieved, the next goal is set. Changes of behaviour can thus be built up to achieve the desired organisational changes.

Box 7.4 Outline of Egan's helping model

Stage 1 The counsellor assists the client to identify and clarify problem situations and unused opportunities.

Step A in this stage is to help clients tell their stories.
Step B consists of helping the client perceive 'blind spots' and look to new perspectives.
Step C consists of finding 'leverage', a way of helping the client to think of change.

Stage 2 Goal-setting: the client is encouraged to develop and choose preferred scenarios.

Step A is to explore possibilities for a new scenario.
Step B is to set an agenda for that scenario.
Step C is to choose which scenario is preferred and to feel commitment to it.

Stage 3 Action: The client moves towards the preferred scenario.

Step A is where the counsellor helps the client to discover strategies for action.
Step B is where the client chooses from the available strategies, to decide which is the 'best fit' for him- or herself.
Step C is where plans are implemented, and valued outcomes are achieved.

Counselling for change is essentially an interactional process. The counsellor never tries to take charge of the situation. The client must always be allowed to retain ownership of his or her own ideas and beliefs, until such time as they choose to modify or change those beliefs. New ideas or beliefs are adopted more easily if they come from the client. The client must be allowed to express anger, whether the anger has been provoked by situations or people. It may possibly be 'displaced' and aimed at the counsellor, as a convenient target; good counsellors are prepared for this. Finally, effective counsellors help clients forsee difficulties which may arise during the implementation stage. Experienced counsellors may be on hand to act as a 'sounding board', to hear about how implementations are proceeding. Change is a risky business – it means leaving what you know for what you don't know. No wonder people are afraid of it!

PROBLEMS OF RESEARCH AND EVALUATION IN ORGANISATIONAL CHANGE

There are many problems in research into organisational change and the evaluation of methods of change. There are so many variables which may cloud issues, for example, type, structure and size of organisation, levels of expertise involved in changes, goals of change, methods of implementing change, and methods of measuring change.

With regard to methods of measuring change, these alone present a number of difficulties. Quantifiable change of items such as costs, productivity, quality and absenteeism can be assessed accurately, but may not present the whole picture. Nicholas (1982) reviewed sixty-four studies which assessed the comparative impact of various changes to these criteria, and concluded that, while many outcomes were favourable, no single method of intervention worked well in all situations. In addition, we must remember that most published analyses tend to be favourable ones; people do not publicise failures!

A meta-analysis was carried out on fifty-six studies of organisational change which used quantitative data (Macy et al., 1986). Overall, they found a positive, significant relationship between interventions and increased productivity, especially within autonomous and semi-autonomous work groups. However, there was a negative relationship between productivity and work involvement, general attitude and satisfaction measures, suggesting that these had declined (see below). Macy and other researchers also noted that many studies on change do not have adequate quantifiable data for inclusion in meta-analyses. There are, of course, always problems with meta-analysis in trying to ensure that groups are comparable and variables have been consistently controlled.

Measuring attitudinal change has always been difficult. Frequently self-report questionnaires are employed, which are scored by using a Likert-type scale[1] However if pre- and post- intervention measures are taken, these may not show improvements in attitude for a number of possible reasons. One may be that, if post-intervention measures are taken too soon, employees may not be completely settled into a new routine, and show resentment at the withdrawal of intervention support. Alternatively, it has been argued (Golembiewski et al., 1976) that ratings declined because participants in the intervention had changed their standards in evaluation. They had undergone a conceptual shift, possibly becoming more critical. This may be why the less tangible elements in Macy's meta-analysis (work satisfaction, involvement and general attitude) were shown to be negatively related to productivity. Productivity may have risen, but standards in the evaluation of attitudes had shifted.

Summary – Organisational Change

All organisations change, in order to keep up to date in their specific fields, to keep abreast of appropriate technology, and to hold on to or improve their share of the market. Dynamics, both within and external to the organisation, necessitate flexibility of management.

Current models suggest that change should be regarded as a process which needs management, rather than simply being allowed to 'happen'. Methods of managing change include the use of training schemes and employee counselling, both of which have produced results acceptable to both employee and organisation. While the use of power to enforce change may be seen as legitimate, it is not usually well received by employees and may therefore be counter-productive. The goals of change may include adaptation to new work practices, increased employee motivation and involvement and increased production. Research into the effectiveness of planned interventions for change is beset with methodological problems, which need to be addressed in order to demonstrate that change can be brought about in a manner satisfactory to both the organisation and its employees.

[1] *Likert-scale:* people responding to a questionnaire are asked to indicate the strength of their response (for example, from 'strongly disagree' to 'strongly agree') on a points scale, usually from 1 to 5 or 1 to 7. Thus gives more information than a yes/no response, and is still easy for the researcher to score.

References

Adams, J.S. (1965) Inequity in social exchange. In Berkowitz, I. (ed) *Advances in Experimental Social Psychology* vol 2. New York: Academic Press.

Alderfer, C.P. (1972) *Existence, Relatedness and Growth: Human Needs in Organisational Settings*. New York: Free Press.

Auerbach S.M. (1989) Stress management and coping research in the health care setting: An overview and methodological commentary. *Journal of Consulting and Clinical Psychology*, 57, 388–395.

Bales, R.F. (1970) *Personality and Interpersonal Behaviour*. New York: Holt, Rinehart and Winston.

Bales, R.F. (1950) *Interaction Process Analysis: A method for the study of small groups*. Cambridge, MA: Addison-Wesley.

Bales, R. F. and Slater, P. (1955) Role differentiation in small decision-making groups. In Parsons, T. et al. (eds) *Family Socialisation and Interaction Process*. New York: Free Press.

Bavelas, A. (1950) Communication patterns in task-oriented groups. *Journal of the Acoustical Society of America*, 2, 725–730.

Beason G. and Belt J.A. (1976) Verifying applicants' backgrounds. *Personnel Journal*, 55, 345–348.

Beck, A.T. (1967) *Depression: Clinical, Experimental and Theoretical Aspects*. New York: Hoeber.

Bethell-Fox, C. (1989) Psychological Testing. In Herriott, P. (ed) *Handbook of Assessment in Organisations*. London: John Wiley.

Bhagat, R.S. and Chassie, M.B. (1981). Determinants of organisational commitment in working women: Some implications for organisational integration. *Journal of Occupational Behaviour*, 2, 17–30.

Biersner, R., Gunderson, E., Ryman, D. and Rahe, R.H. (1971) Correlations of physical fitness, perceived health status and dispensary visits with performance in stressful training. *USN Medical Neuropsychiatric Research Unit, Technical Report No. 71–30*. Washington, DC: US Navy.

Bower, J.L. and Weinberg, M.W. (1988) Statecraft, strategy and corporate leadership. *California Management Review*, 30, 39–56.

Broadbent, D.E. (1971) *Decision and Stress*. New York: Academic Press.

Bromet, E., Dew, M., Parkinson, D.K. and Schulbert, H. (1988) Predictive effects on occupational and marital stress on the mental health of a male workforce. *Journal of Organisational Behaviour*, 9, 1–13.

Brunner, E.J., Marmot, M.G. White, I.R., O'Brien, J.R., Etherington, M.D., Slavin, B.M., Kearney, E.M. and Smith, G.D. (1993) Gender and employment grade differences in blood cholesterol, apolipoproteins and haemostaitic factors in the Whitehall II study. *Atherosclerosis*, (Sept.), 102 (2), 195–207.

Burns, T. and Stalker, T.M. (1961) *The Management of Innovation*. London: Tavistock.

Cascio, W.F. (1978, new edition 1991) *Applied Psychology in Personnel Management*. Reston, VA: Reston.

Chaterjee, D.S. (1987) Repetition strain injury – a recent review. *Journal of the Society of Occupational Medicine*, 37, 100–105.

Chaterjee, D.S. (1992) Workplace upper limb disorders: a prospective study with intervention. *Journal of the Society of Occupational Medicine*, 42, 129–136.

Cohen, S. (1983) Effects and after-effects of stress or expectations. *Journal of Personality and Social Psychology*, 45 (6), 1243–1254.

Cohen, S. (1986) Contrasting Hassles Scale and Perceived Stress Scale: who's really measuring appraised stress? *American Psychologist*, 41 (6), 716–718.

Coleman, J., Butcher, J. and Carson, R.C. (1980) *Abnormal Psychology and Modern Life*, 6th edition. Glenview: Scott Foresman.

Conger, J.A. and Kanungo (1987) Toward and behavioural theory of charismatic leadership. *Academy of Management Review*, 12, 637–647.

Cooper, C.L. and Hensman, R. (1985) A comparative investigation of executive stress: a ten-nation study. *Stress Medicine*, 1, 295–301.

Cooper, C.L. (1995) Report of IPD Conference, Harrowgate. In *People Management*, IPD, 2 November.

Cooper, C.L. and Hingley, P. (1985) *The Change Makers*. London: Harper and Row.

Cox, T. (1993) Stress research and stress management: Putting theory to work.

HSE Contract Research Report, No. 61, HMSO.

Cox, T. (1980). Repetitive work. In Cooper, C.L. and Payne, R. (eds) *Current Concerns in Occupational Stress*. Chichester: Wiley.

Cox, T., Watts, Co and Barnett, A. (1981) The experience and effects of task-inherent demand. *Final technical report to the US Army Research, Development and Standardisation Group, UK.*

Cox, S., Cox, T., Thirlaway, M. and Mackay, C.J. (1985) Effects of simulated repetitive work on urinary catecholamine excretion. *Ergonomics*, 25, 1129–1141.

Cox, T. and Leather, P. (1994). The prevention of violence at work: application of a cognitive behavioural theory. In Cooper, C.L. and Robertson, I. (eds) *International Review of Industrial and Organisational Psychology*. Chichester: Wiley.

Cromie, S. (1981). Women as managers in Northern Ireland. *Journal of Occupational Psychology*, 54 (2), 87–91.

Cronbach, L.J. (1955) Processes affecting scores on understanding others and assumed similarity. *Psychological Bulletin* 52, 177–193.

Czeisler, C.A., Moore, E., Martin, C. and Coleman, R. (1982). *Science*, 217 (4558), 460–463.

DeLongis, A., Coyne, J.C., Dakof, G., Folkman, S. and Lazarus, R.S. (1982) Relationship of daily hassles, uplifts and major life events to health status. *Health Psychology*, 1 (2), 119–136.

Dobson, P. (1989). Reference Reports. In Herriott, P. (ed) *Assessment and Selection in Organisations*. Chichester: Wiley.

Dohrenwend, B.S., Krasnoff, L. Askenasy, A. and Dohrenwend, B.P. (1988) The Psychiatric Epidemiology Research Interview Life Events Scale. In Goldberg, L. and Breznitz, S. (eds) *Handbook of Stress: Theoretical and Clinical Aspects*. New York: Free Press.

Drakeley, R. (1989) Biographical Data. In Herriott, P. (ed) *Assessment and Selection in Organisations*. Chichester: Wiley.

Dunham, R., Pierce, J.L. and Castenada, M.B. (1987) Alternative work schedules: two field quasi-experiments. *Personnel Psychology*, 40, 215–242.

Dunnette, M.D., Campbell, J.P. and Hakel, M.D. (1967) Factors contributing to job satisfaction and dissatisfaction and in six occupational groups. *Organisational Behaviour and Human Performance*, 2, 143–174.

Egan, G. (1994) *The Skilled Helper: A Problem Management Approach to Helping* (5th edition). Pacific Grove, CA: Brooks Cole.

Erez, M. and Arad, R. (1986) Participative goal-setting: social, motivational and cognitive factors. *Journal of Applied Psychology*, 71, 591–597.

Erez, M. and Zidon, I. (1984) Effect of goal acceptance on the relationship of goal difficulty to performance. *Journal of Applied Psychology*, 69, 69–78.

Feather, N.T. (1992). *The Psychological Impact of Unemployment*. New York: Springer-Verlag.

Feldman, D. C. (1984). The development and enforcement of group norms. *Academy of Management Review*, 9, 47–53.

Fiedler, F.E. (1967) *A Theory of Leadership Effectiveness*. New York: McGraw-Hill.

Fine, B. (1963) Introversion-extroversion and motor vehicle driver behaviour. *Perceptual and Motor Skills*, 12, 95–100.

Finlay-Jones, R.A. (1988) Life events and psychiatric illness. In Henderson, A.S. and Burrows, G.D. (ed) *Handbook of Social Psyamatry*. Amsterdam: Elsevier.

French, J.R.P. and Caplan, R.D. (1972) Organisational stress and individual strain. In Marrow, A. (ed) *The Failure of Success*. New York: AMACOM.

French, J.R.P., Caplan, R.D. and Van Harrison, R. (1982) *The Mechanisms of Job Stress and Strain*. New York: Wiley.

French, J.R.P. and Raven, B. (1959) The bases of social power. In Cartwright, D. (ed) *Studies in Social Power*. Ann Arbor, MI: Institute of Social Research.

Friedman, M. and Rosenman, R.H. (1974) *Type A Behaviour and Your Heart*. New York: Knopf.

Furnham, A. (1992) *Personality at Work*. London: Routledge.

Gaines, J. and Jermier, J.M. (1983) Emotional exhaustion in a high-stress organisation. *Academy of Management Journal*, 26, 567–586.

Galbraith, J. (1973) *Designing Complex Organisations*. Menlo Park, CA: Addison Wesley.

Gannon, M.J., Noreland, D. and Robeson, F.E. (1983) Shift work has complex effects on lifestyles and work habits. *Personnel Administrator*, 28 (5), 93–97.

Ganster, D.C. and Fusilier, M.R. (1989).

Control in the workplace. In Cooper, C.L. and Robertson, I. (eds) *International Review of Industrial and Organisational Psychology*. Chichester: Wiley.

Ganster, D.C., Fusilier, M.R. and Mayes, B.T. (1986) Role of social support in the experience of stress at work. *Journal of Applied Psychology*, 71, 102–110.

Golembiewski, R.T., Billingsley, K. and Yeager, S. (1976) Measuring change and persistence in human affairs: types of change generated by OD designs. *Journal of Applied Behavioural Science*, 12, 133–157.

Gorlin, H. (1982) An overview of corporate personnel practices. *Personnel Journal*, 61, 125–130.

Greenberg, J., Solomon, S., Pyszcynxki, T., Rosenblatt, A., Burling, J., Lyon, D., Simon, L. and Pinel, E. (1992) Why do people need self-esteem? Converging evidence that self-esteem serves an anxiety-buffering function. *Journal of Personality and Social Psychology*, 63 (6), 913–922.

Halpin, A.W. and Winer, B.J. (1957) A factorial study of the leader behaviour descriptions. In Stogdill, R.M. and Coons, A.E. (eds) *Leader Behaviour: its Description and Measurement*. Columbus: Ohio State University Bureau of Business Research.

Hamner, W.C. (1974) Reinforcement theory and contingency management in organisational settings. In Tosi, H.L. and Hamner, W.C. (eds) *Organizational Behaviour and Management: a Contingency Approach*. Chicago: St Clair Press.

Hansen, C.P. (1989) A causal model of the relationship among accidents, biodata, personality and cognitive factors. *Journal of Applied Psychology*, 74, 81–90.

Henderson, S. (1981) Social relationships, adversity and neurosis: an analysis of prospective observations. *British Journal of Psychiatry*, 138, 391–398.

Herriott, P. (1989) The selection interview. In Herriott, P. (ed) *Assessment and Selection in Organisations*. Chichester; Wiley

Herzberg, F., Mausner, B. and Snyderman, B.B. (1959) *The Motivation to Work*. New York: Wiley.

Herzberg, F. (1968). One more time: how do you motivate employees? *Harvard Business Review*, 52–62.

Hill, G.W. (1982) Group versus individual performances. Are N+1 heads better than one? *Psychological Bulletin*, 89, 517–539.

Hirschorn, L. (1987) *The Workplace Within*. Cambridge, MA: MIT Press.

Hollander, E.P. and Offerman, L.R. (1990) The relational features of organisational leadership and followship. In Clark, K. and Clark, M. (ed) *Measures of Leadership*. West Drange, NJ: Leadership Library of America.

Holmes, T.H. and Rahe, R.H. (1967) Social Readjustment Rating Scale. *Journal of Psychosomatic Research*, 11, 213–218.

House, R.J. (1971) A path-goal theory of leader effectiveness. *Administrative Science Quarterly*, 16, 321–338.

House, Spangler and Woycke (1989) Working paper.

Hunter J. and Hunter, R.(1984) Validity and utility of alternative predictors of job performance. *Psychological Bulletin*, 96, 72–98.

Indvik, J. (1986) Path-goal theory of leadership: a meta-analysis. Presented at the meeting of the Academy of Management, Chicago.

Ivancevich, J.M., Matteson, M.T., Freedman, S. and Phillips, J.S. (1990) Worksite stress mangement interventions. *American Journal of Health Promotions*, 12–23.

Ivancevich, J.M. and McMahon, J.T. (1982) The effects of goal-setting, external feedback and self-generated feedback on outcome variables. *Academy of Management Journal*, 25 (2), 359–372.

Ivancevich, J.M., Matteson, M.T. and Preston, C. (1982) Occupational stress, Type A behaviour and physical well-being. *Academy of Management Journal*, 25, 373–391.

Jackson, S.E., Turner, J.A. and Brief, A.P. (1987) Correlates of burnout among public service lawyers. *Journal of Occupational Behaviour*, 8, 339–349.

Janis, I.L. (1972) *Victims of Groupthink*. Boston: Houghton Mifflin.

Jermier, J.M., Gaines, J. and McIntosh, N.J. (1989). Reaction to physically dangerous work: a conceptual and empirical analysis. *Journal of Organisational Behaviour*, 10, 15–33.

Karasek, R.A. (1979) Job demands, job decision latitude and mental strain: implications for job redesign.

Administrative Science Quarterly, 24, 285–308.

Karasek, R.A., Schwartz, J. and Theorell, T. (1982) *Job Characteristics, Occupation and Coronary Heart Disease* (Final report no. R-01-OH00906). Cincinnati OH: National Institute for Occupational Safety and Health.

Karasek, R.A. and Theorell, T. (1990) *Healthy Work: Stress, Productivity and the Reconstruction of Working Life*. New York: Basic Books.

Kasl, S.V. and Cobb, S. (1982) Variability of stress effects among men experiencing job loss. In Goldberger, L. and Breznitz, S. (eds) *Handbook of Stress: Theoretical and Clinical Aspects*. New York: Free Press.

Katz, D. and Kahn, R.L. (1978) *The Social Psychology of Organisations*, 2nd edn. New York: Wiley.

Kerr, S. and Jermier, J.M. (1978) Substitutes for leadership: their meaning and measurement. *Organisational Behaviour and Human Performance*, 22, 375–404.

Kinicki A, and Lockwood, C. (1985) The Interview Process. *Journal of Vocational Behaviour*, 26, 117–25.

Kobasa, S., Maddi, S. and Kahn, S. (1982) Hardiness and health: a prospective study. *Journal of Personality and Social Psychology*, 42, 168–177.

Kohjasten, M. (1993). Motivating private versus public sector managers. *Public Personnel Management*, 22 (3), 391–401.

Kotter, J.P. (1982) *The General Managers*. New York: Free Press.

Latham, G and Saari L. (1984) Do people do what they say? Further studies on the situational interview. *Journal of Applied Psychology* 69, 569–73.

Lawler, E.E. and Porter, L.W. (1967) The effect of performance on satisfaction. *Industrial Relations*, 7, 20–28.

Lawrence, P.R. and Lorsch, J. (1967) *Organisation and Environment*. Cambridge, MA: Harvard University Press.

Lazarus, R.S. (1976) *Patterns of Adjustment*. New York: McGraw-Hill.

Lazarus, R.S. and Folkman, S. (1984) *Stress, Appraisal and Coping*. New York: Springer Publications.

Leavitt, H.J. (1951) Some effects of certain communication patterns on group performance. *Journal of Abnormal and Social Psychology*, 46, 38–50.

Leavitt, H.J. (1964) Applied organisation change in industry: Structural, technological and human approaches. In Cooper, W.W. *New Perspectives in Organisation Research*. New York: Wiley.

Levine, E.L., Ash, R.A., Hall, H. and Sistrunk, F. (1983). Evaluation of job analysis methods by experienced job analysts. *Academy of Management Journal*, 26, 339–347.

Lewin, K. (1947) Group decision and social change. In Newcomb, T. and Hartley, E. (eds) *Readings in Social Psychology*. New York: Holt, Rhinehart and Winston.

Lewin, K., Lippitt, R. and White, R.K. (1939) Patterns of aggressive behaviour in experimentally created social climates. *Journal of Social Psychology*, 10, 271–279.

Likert, R. (1961) *New Patterns of Management*. New York: McGraw-Hill.

Likert, R. (1967) *The Human Organisation*. New York: McGraw-Hill.

Locke, E.A. (1968) Towards a theory of task motivation and incentives. *Organisational Behaviour and Human Performance*, 3, 157–189.

Locke, E.A., Shaw, K.N., Saari, L.M. and Latham, G.P. (1981) Goal-setting and task performance: 1969–1980. *Psychological Bulletin*, 90, 125–152.

Mackworth, N. (1948) The breakdown of vigilance during prolonged visual search. *Quarterly Journal of Experimental Psychology*, 1, 5–61.

Macy, B.A., Hurts, C.C.M., Izumi, H. Norton, L.W. and Smith, R.R. (1986) Presented at the National Academy of Management 46th Annual Meeting, Chicago, Illinois, 101.

Margolis, B. and Kroes, W. (1974) Work and the health of man. In O'Toole, J. (ed) *Work and the Quality of Life*. Cambridge, MA: MIT Press.

Martin and Peterson, M. (1987)Two-tier wage structures: implications for equity theory. *Academy of Management Journal*, 30 (2), 297–315.

Maslach, C. and Jackson, S.E. (1981) The measurement of experienced burnout. *Journal of Occupational Behaviour*, 2, 99–113.

Maslow, A. H. (1970) *Motivation and Personality* (2nd edition). New York: Harper and Row.

Mastrofski, S., Ritti, R. and Snipes, J. (1994). Expectancy theory and police productivity in DVI enforcement. *Law*

Society Review, 28 (1), 113–148.

Matteson, M. and Ivancevich, J.M. (1982) The how, what and why of stress management training. *Personnel Journal*, 61 (10), 768–774.

Mayo, E. (1933) *The Human Problems of an Industrial Civilization*. Cambridge: Harvard University Press.

McClelland, D.C. (1961) *The Achieving Society*. Princeton: Van Nostrand.

McClelland, D.C. and Boyatzis, R.E. (1982) Leadership motive pattern and long-term success in management. *Journal of Applied Psychology*, 67, 737–743.

McCormick, I.A. and Cooper, C.L. (1988) Executive stress: extending the international comparison. *Human Relations*, 41, 65–72.

McCormick, I.A., Jeanneret, P.R. and Meacham, R.C. (1972) A study of job characteristics and job dimensions as based on the Position Analysis Questionnaire (PAQ). *Journal of Applied Psychology*, 56, 347–368.

McDonald, L.M. and Korabik, K. (1991). Sources of stress and ways of coping among male and female managers. *Journal of Social Behaviour and Personality*, 6 (7), 185–198.

McGregor, D.M. (1957) The human side of enterprise. *Adventure in thought and action: proceedings of the fifth anniversary convocation of the School of Industrial Management, MIT.* Cambridge, MA: MIT Press.

Meese, G.B., Lewis, M.I., Wyon, D.P. & Kok, P. (1984), A laboratory study of the effects of moderate thermal stress on the performance of factory workers. *Ergonomics*, 27, 19–43.

Milgram, S. (1963). A behavioural study of obedience. *Journal of Abnormal and Social Psychology*, 67, 371–378.

Miner, J.B. (1983) The unpaved road from theory: over the mountains to application. In Kilmann, R.H., Thomas, K.W., Slevin, D.P., Naith, R. and Jerrel, S.L. (eds) *Producing Useful Knowledge for Organisations*. New York: Praeger.

Miner, J.B. (1984) The unpaved road over the mountains: from theory to applications. *The Industrial/Organizational Psychologist*, 21, 9–20.

Mosel J. and Goheen, H. (1982) Agreement amongst replies to an employment recommendation questionnaire. *American Psychologist*, 7, 365–336.

Murphy, L.R. (1988) Workplace interventions for stress reduction and prevention. In Cooper, C.L. and Payne, R. (eds) *Causes, Coping and Consequences of Stress at Work*. New York: McGraw-Hill.

Nash, A. and Carroll, S. (1970) A hard look at the reference check. *Business Horizons*, 13, 43–49.

Nicholas, J.M. (1982) The comparative impact of organisation development interventions on hard criteria measures. *Academy of Management Review*, 9, 531–4.

Nord, W.R. (1989) OD's unfulfilled vision: Some lessons from economics. In Woodman, R. and Pasmore, W.A. (eds) *Research in Organisational Change and Development*, Vol.3, Greenwich, CT: SAI Prest.

Noyes, J., Starr, and Rankin (1996) Human error in aviation: designing warning systems from a user perspective. In proceedings of IEE Colloquim '*Control rooms, cockpits and command centres*', Digest 1996. London: Institution of Electrical Engineers.

Oldham, G.R. (1988) Effects of changes in workspace partitions and spatial density on employee reactions: a quasi-experiment. *Journal of Applied Psychology*, 73, 253–258.

Ormel, J., Sanderman, R. and Stewart, R. (1989) Personality as a modifier of life events distress relationship: a longitudinal structural equation model. *Personality and Individual Differences*, 9 (6), 973–982.

Owens, W.A. and Schoenfeldt, L.F. (1979) Towards a classification of persons. *Journal of Applied Psychology Monograph*, 65, 569–607.

Paton, D. (1990) Assessing the impact of disaster on helpers. *Counselling Psychology Quarterly*, 3 (2), 149–152.

Perry, L. (1993) Effects of inequity on job satisfaction and self-evaluation in a national sample of African-American workers. *Journal of Social Psychology*, 133 (4), 565–573.

Peters, L.H., Hartke, D.D. and Pohlmann, J.T. (1985) Fiedler's Contingency Theory of leadership: an application of the meta-analysis procedures of Schmidt and Hunter. *Psychological Bulletin*, 97, 274–285.

Pfeffer, P. and Shapiro, S.J. (1978) Personnel

differences in male and female MBA candidates. *Business Quarterly*, 43, 77–80.

Porras, J. and Silvers, R.C. (1991) Organisational development and transformation. *American Review of Psychology*, 42, 51–78.

Porter, M. (1990) *The Competitive Advantage of Nations*. London: Macmillan.

Powell, G.N. (1988). *Women and Men in Management*. Newbury Park, CA: Sage.

Prieto, J. (1989) Tests of aptitude. In Herriott, P. (ed) *Assessment and Selection in Organisations*. Chichester: Wiley.

Rauschenberger, J., Schmitt, N. and Hunter, J.E. (1980) A test of the need hierachy concept by a Markov model of change in need strength. *Administrative Science Quarterly*, 25, 654–670.

Reilly, R. and Chao, G. (1982) Validity and fairness of some alternative employee selection procedures. *Personnel Psychology*, 33, 1–62.

Rosenbaum, L.L. and Rosenbaum, W.B. (1971) Morale and productivity consequences of group leadership style, stress and type of task. *Journal of Applied Psychology*, 55, 343–348.

Rotter, J.B. (1966) Generalised expectancies for internal versus external control of reinforcement. *Psychological Monographs*, 30 (1), 1–26.

Sadler, P. (1989) Management development. In Sissons, K. (ed) *Personnel Management in Britain*. Oxford: Blackwell.

Sauter, S., Murphy, L. and Hurrell, J. (1992) Prevention of work-related psychological disorders: A national strategy proposed by the National Institute for Occupational Safety and Health. In Keita. G. and Sauter, S. (eds) *Work and Well-Being: An Agenda for the 1990s*. Washington, DC: American Psychological Association.

Schein, E.H. (1987) *The Clinical Perspective in Fieldwork*. Beverley Hills, CA: Sage.

Schein, E.H. (1990) Organisational culture. *American Psychologist*, Feb., 109–119.

Schneider, B. (1987) The people make the place. *Personnel Psychology*, 40, 437–53.

Schneider, J. and Locke, E.A. (1971) A critique of Herzberg's incident classification system and a suggested revision. *Organizational Behaviour and Human Performance*, 6, 441–457.

Selye, H. (1956) *The Stress of Life*. New York: McGraw-Hill.

Shaw, M.E. (1954) Some effects of problem complexity upon problem solution in different communication nets. *Journal of Experimental Psychology*, 48, 211–217.

Shirom, A. (1989) Burnout in work organisations. In Cooper, C.L. and Robertson, I. (eds.) *International Review of Industrial and Organisational Psychology*, 1989, Chichester: Wiley.

Shouksmith, G. and Burrough, S. (1988) Job stress factors for New Zealand and Canadian air-traffic controllers. *Applied Psychology: An International Review*, 37 (3), 263–270.

Skinner, B.F. (1938) *Science and Human Behaviour*. New York: Macmillan.

Smith, A.P. (1995) Determinants of human performance in organizational settings. In Cooper, C.L. and Robertson, I.T. (eds) *International Review of Industrial and Organisational Psychology*. Chichester: Wiley.

Spector, P.E., (1987) Interactive effects of perceived control and job stressors on alterative and health outcomes for clerical workers. *Work and Stress*, 1, 155–162.

Spector, P.E., Dwyer, D.J. and Jex, S.M. (1988) Relation of job stressors to affective, health and performance outcomes: a comparison of multiple data sources. *Journal of Applied Psychology*, 73, 11–19.

Steers, R.M. and Porter, L.W. (1979, 2nd edition; 1983, 3rd edition) *Motivation and Work Behaviour*. New York: McGraw-Hill.

Stogdill, R.M. (1974) *Handbook of Leadership: A Survey of Theory and Research*. New York: Free Press.

Stoner, J.A.F. (1961) A comparison of individual and group decisions involving risk. Unpublished Masters thesis. Cambridge, MA: MIT.

Szilagyi, A.D. and Wallace, M.J. (1990) *Organisational Behaviour and Performance*. Scott-Foresman.

Tajfel, H. (1981) *Human Group and Social Categories*. Cambridge: Cambridge University Press.

Tajfel, H., Billig, M.G, Bundy, R.P. and Flament, C. (1971) Social categorisation and intergroup behaviour. *European Journal of Social Psychology*, 1 (2), 149–178.

Taylor, F.W. (1916) The principles of scientific management. Originally published in *Bulletin of the Taylor Society*. Reprinted in

Mankin, D., Ames, R. and Grodsky, M. (eds) (1980) *Classics of Industrial and Organisational Psychology.* Oak Park IL: Moore.

Tennant, C. (1983) Life events and pscyhological morbidity: the evidence from prospective studies. *Psychology Medicine*, 13, 483–486.

Thompson, S.C. (1981) Will it hurt less if I can control it? A complex answer to a simple question. *Psychological Bulletin*, 90 (1), 89–101.

Tichy, N.M. and Devanna, M.A. (1986) The transformational leader. *Training and Development Journal*, 40 (7), 27–32.

van der Pompe, G. and de Heus, P. (1993). Work stress, social support, and strains among male and female managers. *Anxiety, Stress and Coping: an International Journal*, 6(3), 215-229.

van Wijck, P. (1994) Evaluating income distributions. *Journal of Economic Psychology*, 15 (1), 173–190.

Vroom,V.H. (1964). *Work and Motivation*. New York: Wiley.

Vroom, V.H. and Mann, F.C. (1960). Leader authoritarianism and employee attitudes. *Personnel Psychology*, 13, 125–140.

Wanous J. (1980) *Organisational Entry*. Reading, MA: Addison-Wesley.

Warr, P. (1990) The measurement of well-being and other aspects of mental health. *Journal of Occupational Psychology*, 63, 193-210.

Warr, P. (1992) Work and mental health: a general model. *MRS/ESRC SAPU Memo* 1382, Sheffield.

Watson, T. (1988) Recruitment and selection. In Sisson, K. (ed) *Personnel Management in Britain*. Oxford: Blackwell.

Watson, D. and Pennebaker, A. (1989) Health complaints, stress and distress: exploring the role of negative affectivity. *Journal of Applied Social Psychology*, 19 (4 Part 2), 831–840.

Weinberg, R.S. (1978) The relationship between intrinsic rewards and intrinsic motivation. *Psychological Reports*, 42 (3), 255–258.

Wickens, C.D. (1992) *Engineering Psychology and Human Performance* (2nd edition). New York: Harper Collins.

Wolfgang, A.P. (1988) Job stress in the health professions: a study of physicians, nurses, and pharmacists. *Behavioural Medicine*, 14, 43–47.

Wolinsky, J. (1982). Beat the clock. *APA Monitor* (Dec.).

Index

Further titles in the *Applying Psychology to...* series are available from Hodder & Stoughton.

0 340 64756 6 **Applying Psychology to Health** by Philip Banyard £6.99
0 340 64392 7 **Applying Psychology to Early Child Development** £6.99
0 340 64758 2 **Applying Psychology to Organisations** by Sheila Hayward £5.99
0 340 64329 3 **Applying Psychology to Education** by Martyn Long £5.99

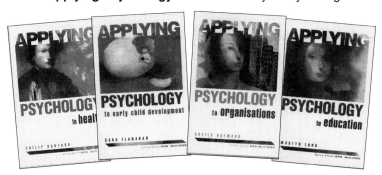

For full details of this series, please call Dan Addelman at Hodder & Stoughton on 0171 873 6272. Look out for forthcoming *Applying Psychology to...* titles, including Sport, the Environment and the Legal World.

All Hodder & Stoughton books are available from your local bookshop or can be ordered direct from the publisher. Just tick the titles you want and fill in the form below. Prices and availability subject to change without notice.

To: Hodder & Stoughton Ltd, Cash Sales Department, Bookpoint, 39 Milton Park, Abingdon, Oxon, OX14 4TD. If you have a credit card you may order by telephone - 01235 400471.

Please enclose a cheque or postal order made payable to Bookpoint Ltd to the value of the cover price and allow the following for postage and packing:
UK and BFPO: £1.00 for the first book, 50p for the second book and 30p for each additional book ordered up to a maximum charge of £3.00.
OVERSEAS & EIRE: £2.00 for the first book, £1.00 for the second book and 50p for each additional book.

Name: _____

Address: _____

If you would prefer to pay by credit card, please complete:

Please debit my Visa/Mastercard/Diner's Card/ American Express (delete as appropriate)

card no: ☐☐☐☐ ☐☐☐☐ ☐☐☐☐ ☐☐☐☐

Signature _____ Expiry date ____ / ____